Sunday Dinner Cookbook

SUNDAY DINNER COOKBOOK

Phyllis S. Prokop

BROADMAN PRESS
Nashville, Tennessee

Library of Congress Catalog Card Number: 69–17897
Dewey Decimal Classification Number: 641.5
Printed in the United States of America
3.Jy69KSP

With much love

and sincere appreciation

this book is dedicated

to my husband

Charles L. Prokop

who

each evening

is jogging a mile

to overcome the effects

of being chief tester

of the recipes

in this book

PREFACE

This is a book for those women who dash in from church each Sunday, hat leaning precariously, Bible and purse in hand, to answer the question, "Mother, what are we having for dinner today?"

As I have prepared and cooked these menus and recipes for a year of Sunday dinners, I have tried to picture you in your kitchen. I have tried to count the number of plates you were placing on the table and to estimate the size of the appetites of those little people coming through the door. I have enjoyed this contact with your family, and I hope you will find equal enjoyment as you read and use the suggestions for Sunday dinners as they appear in this book.

I have tried to select recipes which you will actually cook, not just read and plan to try someday. As they appear, the recipes are for families of four to six members, but they can be doubled or tripled at will. I have tried to keep in mind that for all of us there are Sundays when the budget is in good condition and Sundays when the primary consideration must be economy.

Doubtless every Christian mother would like to leave her children with memories of happy, relaxed Sundays. It is my sincere desire that this book will help you to plan your Sunday dinners in such a way that your day, and consequently your family's day, will be more relaxed and happy. In so doing, our attitudes will be more conducive to that which is most important—the study and understanding of God's Word.

Acknowledgments

I wish to express my appreciation and sincere thanks to: my dear friends in Houston, Texas; New Orleans, Mandeville, and Covington, Louisiana; Weleetka, Beggs, Broken Arrow, and Oklahoma City, Oklahoma; and elsewhere, who have contributed recipes, thoughts, and enthusiasm to the preparation of this book;

Janey Guest, who has brought to the book a background in home economics and many pleasant hours of conversation;

Charles Kent Prokop, who has given me the benefit of his college-freshman wisdom and has littered the floor of my study with written bits which he has evaluated by saying, "Yes, Mother, I get it, but do you really think it's worth it?"

B. Kimball Prokop, who has provided constant practical, if not esthetic, encouragement by saying, "Mother, I'm starving!"

PHYLLIS S. PROKOP

❧✖ MENU ✖❧

1

Chicken Breasts in Sour
  Cream
Cranberry Sauce Mold
  Buttered Broccoli
Frances' Peach Loaf

Hot Rolls with Butter
Coffee, Tea, or Milk

Fix-Ahead Instructions

1. Depending on your cooking facilities, place chicken in oven as directed and set oven on automatic timer to cook 1½ hours; or, cook in oven for 1¼ hours before you leave for church. Leave out, allowing it to come to room temperature while you are away. Return to oven for 20 more minutes when you return from church.
2. Prepare salad mold the day before.
3. Prepare peach loaf up to 3 days before serving, and refrigerate. Do not add whipped cream topping until just before serving.

Chicken Breasts in Sour Cream

4 chicken breasts
1 can (3 oz.) mushrooms, drained
1 can mushroom soup, undiluted
1 cup sour cream
paprika

Arrange chicken in shallow buttered baking dish so pieces do not overlap. Cover with mushrooms. Add well-blended mushroom soup and sour cream. This will completely cover chicken. Sprinkle with paprika and cook uncovered 1½ to 2 hours at 350°. The chicken will be covered with a golden-brown sauce when done.

Cranberry Sauce Mold

1 small pkg. cherry gelatin
1 can cranberry sauce, jellied style
1 pkg. (3 oz.) cream cheese

Prepare gelatin as directed on package. Add room-temperature cream cheese and beat until blended. Cut cranberry sauce into squares (roughly ½ inch) and add to gelatin mixture. Mix lightly. Pour into mold and refrigerate.

Buttered Broccoli

Prepare frozen broccoli as directed on package. Season with butter.

Frances' Peach Loaf

3 egg whites, beaten stiffly
1 cup sugar
¼ tsp. baking powder
1 tsp. vanilla
20 Ritz crackers, crumbled
½ cup nuts, chopped

Topping

1 can (2 cups)
   sliced peaches, drained
½ pint whipping cream

Add sugar slowly to beaten egg whites. Add baking powder, vanilla, and Ritz crackers. Add nuts. Place in small loaf pan and bake at 350° for 30 minutes. Cool. Before serving, slice and top with peaches and whipped cream.

⇨⊱❈ MENU ❈⊰⇦

2

"How imposing it would be if pumpkins grew upon a tree," wrote Guy Westmore Carryl. I think you will find "Ann's Pumpkin Cake" almost this imposing. Remember it for special Sundays from September through Christmas.

Menu

Colby's Spiced Chicken over
   Rice
Spinach-stuffed Onions
Cucumber and Pear Salad
   with Sour Cream
Ann's Pumpkin Cake

Rolls and Butter
Coffee, Tea, or Milk

Fix-Ahead Instructions

1. The chicken can be prepared days ahead, refrigerated or frozen, and heated just before serving. Prepare instant rice while chicken is heating.
2. Prepare salad mold a day ahead and unmold Sunday morning while you are preparing breakfast.
3. Prepare "Spinach-stuffed Onions" the day before. Allow to come to room temperature while you are at church. Place in oven to heat for 10 to 15 minutes at 300° before serving.
4. Bake pumpkin cake. It will stay moist for several days if wrapped well. It also freezes well.

Colby's Spiced Chicken

1 stick margarine
2 fryers, cut up
2 medium onions
1 clove garlic
1 bay leaf

1 tsp. thyme
2 T chopped parsley
1 can (6 oz.) mushrooms,
   plus liquid

In large pot, brown chicken in margarine for about 10 minutes. Add chopped onions, garlic, mushrooms, and seasonings. Cook over low fire 1 hour. Keep pot tightly covered. Do not add more water. Serve on bed of instant rice prepared according to directions on package.

Spinach-stuffed Onions

1 medium onion
   per person
2 T margarine
1 T flour
1 cup milk

1 pkg. frozen chopped spinach, cooked
2 hard-boiled eggs
½ cup cracker crumbs
½ tsp. salt

Boil whole onions until tender. Cool and carefully remove centers, leaving an onion cup. Reserve centers. In separate pan melt 2 tablespoons margarine. Add 2 tablespoons flour and blend. When combined, add 1 cup milk and cook to make smooth sauce. Add to sauce the package of heated spinach, the inside portions of onions, finely chopped eggs, cracker crumbs, and salt and pepper to taste. Mix. Fill onion cups with this mixture. Serve hot.

Cucumber and Pear Salad with Sour Cream

1 small pkg. lime gelatin
1 large cucumber
6 pear halves, cut in pieces
½ cup sour cream

Prepare gelatin according to directions on package. Add thick slices of cucumber and pieces of pear. Chill. Serve on lettuce with sour cream dressing.

Ann's Pumpkin Cake

3 cups sugar
1 cup shortening,
   room temperature
3 eggs, beaten slightly
1 can (2 cups) pumpkin
1 tsp. vanilla
3 cups flour

½ tsp. baking powder
¼ tsp. salt
1 tsp. cloves
1 tsp. nutmeg
1 tsp. soda
1 tsp. cinnamon
1 tsp. allspice

Cream shortening and sugar. Add beaten eggs, pumpkin, and vanilla. Sift dry ingredients together and add to creamed mixture. Mix. Bake in 10-inch tube pan or Bundt pan for 1¼ hours. Set oven for 350°.

❧❂❧ MENU ❂❧

3

This one is for the day you need something simple, quick, and economical. Everything but the cake can be done after you return from church.

Menu

Oven Tuna

Pimiento Corn

Apple Celery Salad

White Cake with Country
    Chocolate Frosting

Brown Bread and Butter

Coffee, Tea, or Milk

Fix-Ahead Instructions

1. Bake and frost cake.

Oven Tuna

2 cans (6½ oz. each) tuna

3 hard-boiled eggs, sliced

1 cup corn flakes, crushed

1 can mushroom soup,
    undiluted

⅓ cup water

Combine all ingredients. Place in greased casserole and bake at 350° about 20 minutes.

Pimiento Corn

To a can of whole kernel corn add 1 small jar pimientos. Add salt and butter to taste.

Apple Celery Salad

3 medium apples
2 cups celery, diced

½ cup nuts
mayonnaise to moisten

Cut unpeeled apples into bite-sized pieces. Add diced celery, nuts, and mayonnaise, and mix lightly.

White Cake with Country Chocolate Frosting

Do you remember when you were a child and went to visit your aunts on a Sunday afternoon? When they served you a slice of cake, the chocolate on top snapped off in little pieces under your fork like chocolate fudge that had been cooked exactly the right length of time. This is the recipe for that frosting.

Cake

Use your favorite white cake mix.

Frosting

2 squares (2 oz.) baking
  chocolate, cut fine
7 T milk
1 T light corn syrup
1½ cups sugar

4 T butter
¼ tsp. salt
1 tsp. vanilla
½ cup nuts

Combine all ingredients except vanilla and nuts. Place over medium heat and bring to a rolling boil. Boil briskly for 1 minute. Cool. Add vanilla and beat to spreading consistency. Add nuts.

➤➤❧ MENU ❧◆◆

4

This is a "down South" dinner for a cold Sunday. Slip the cornbread into the oven while the other foods are warming, and you are ready.

Menu

Elwyn's Favorite Chicken
  and Okra Stew
Black-eyed Peas
Pecan Pie

Mexican Cornbread
Coffee, Tea, or Milk

Fix-Ahead Instructions

1. Cook stew. Heat before serving.
2. Cook black-eyed peas. Heat before serving.
3. Measure and combine all dry ingredients for cornbread. Measure and combine all liquid ingredients for cornbread. When you return from church, combine, mix, and bake.
4. Bake pecan pie.

Elwyn's Favorite Chicken and Okra Stew

1 fryer, cut into pieces
3 T margarine
1 can (2 cups) tomatoes with liquid
1 pkg. (10 oz.) frozen whole okra
salt to taste

Brown chicken in margarine. Add tomatoes with liquid and salt. Add frozen okra. Allow to simmer about 1 hour. To serve, arrange in large bowl or on platter with chicken pieces around edge. This is very colorful and good. "You-all" down South will like it.

Black-eyed Peas

3 slices bacon
1 onion, chopped
½ bell pepper, chopped
1 can or frozen pkg. black-eyed peas

Cook bacon until limp. Add onion and pepper and sauté. Add peas. If you are using canned peas, simmer for about 10 minutes. If you are using frozen peas, follow directions on package for cooking. Then add them to the seasoning mixture and cook over low heat for 5 minutes.

Mexican Cornbread

1 cup cornmeal, as coarse as you can find
1 can cream-style corn
¾ cup buttermilk
½ cup grated cheese
1 small can El Chico green peppers, chopped, plus liquid
1 tsp. salt
½ tsp. soda
1 T bacon drippings
1 small onion, minced

Combine all ingredients and mix. Pour into very hot iron skillet which has been well greased. Bake about 45 minutes at 375°.

Pecan Pie

1 unbaked pie shell

1 cup brown sugar	3 eggs, beaten
¼ cup flour	¼ tsp. salt
1 T margarine	1 tsp. vanilla
1 cup light corn syrup	1 cup pecan halves

Mix sugar and flour. Cream with margarine. Add syrup and beaten eggs. Beat until foamy. Add salt, vanilla, and pecan halves. Pour into 9-inch unbaked pie shell. Bake at 325° about 40 minutes.

Eddie's Garlic Cheese Grits

1 cup grits, quick cooking
½ stick margarine
1 round stick garlic cheese
1 egg

(This dish is not included in the menu but I wanted to give it to you in case you are a real Southerner looking for a new grits recipe.) Cook quick grits as directed on package. Add margarine and cheese and mix well. Add one egg and mix. Bake in greased casserole 30 minutes at 350°.

-→❋❋ MENU ❋❋←-

5

I like this menu for a very special dinner. Allow 30 minutes oven time for the "Turkey Amandine" while you are serving small cups of soup. Heat the English peas and take the salad from the refrigerator. The dessert is ready, waiting to be sliced.

Menu

Corn Celery Soup with
   Crackers
Turkey Amandine with Broc-
   coli
English Peas
Dorothy's Fresh Fruit Salad
Superb Cheese Cake

Hot Rolls and Butter
Coffee, Tea, or Milk

Fix-Ahead Instructions

1. Prepare soup.
2. Prepare "Turkey Amandine" and have it ready to slip into the oven.
3. Prepare fruits for salad.
4. Prepare and bake cheese cake. Refrigerate.

Corn Celery Soup with Crackers

1 can cream-style corn
1 can cream of celery soup
1 soup can milk

Combine and heat. Serve with crackers.

Turkey Amandine with Broccoli

4 ozs. noodles, cooked
1 pkg. frozen broccoli
   spears, cooked
2 T margarine
2 T flour
1 cup evaporated milk
2 cups turkey broth

1 tsp. monosodium glutamate
1 tsp. Worcestershire sauce
2 cups cooked turkey, diced
½ tsp. salt
¼ cup toasted slivered
   almonds

Cook and drain noodles. Place in buttered casserole.
Cut cooked broccoli in 1-inch pieces. Reserve 1 broccoli blossom to garnish top. Arrange broccoli on bed of noodles. In separate pan combine margarine, flour, and liquids, and cook until slightly thickened. Add seasonings and turkey. Pour turkey mixture over noodles and broccoli. Place broccoli blossom on top. Sprinkle with almonds. Bake at 350° for 30 minutes.

English Peas

Prepare frozen peas as directed on package.

Dorothy's Fresh Fruit Salad

2 grapefruit, peeled and sectioned
3 oranges, peeled and sectioned
1 can pineapple bits, drained
1 banana, sliced

Ahead of time prepare grapefruit sections, orange sections, and drain pineapple bits. Before serving, combine fruits. Add sliced banana. Add your favorite dressing, or "Fruit Dressing" from recipe below:

Fruit Dressing

¼ cup cream   ½ tsp. salt
⅛ tsp. ginger   juice of ½ lemon

Mix cream with ginger and salt. Add lemon juice slowly, mixing well.

Superb Cheese Cake

This cheese cake is very good and also very easy to prepare. But I must confess it is not inexpensive, so try it some week when the budget is in good condition.

Graham Cracker Shell

(You may buy a shell already prepared or use the following recipe.)

20 graham crackers
½ stick margarine (let soften to room temperature)
¼ cup sugar

Combine ingredients and press into pie pan.

Filling

2 pkgs. (8 oz. each) cream   ½ cup sugar
  cheese   1 tsp. vanilla
2 eggs

Soften cream cheese and mix other ingredients with it thoroughly. Put in graham cracker shell and bake about 20 minutes at 350°. Allow to cool. Add topping.

Topping

1 cup sour cream
2 T sugar
¼ tsp. vanilla

Combine ingredients and spread over cooled pie. Refrigerate. Serve in small slices.

21

➤➤✦ MENU ✦◄◄

6

"Even a king wears only one crown."
Application: If you knock yourself out on the entrée, you may relax on the dessert.

Menu

Vivian's Beef Stroganoff
  in Nest of Noodles
Marinated Green Bean Salad
White Mountain Relish Plate
Ice Cream

Bread and Butter
Coffee, Tea, or Milk

Fix-Ahead Instructions

1. Prepare the Stroganoff mixture ahead, but do not add sour cream until time to heat just before serving.
2. Prepare marinated green beans the day before and refrigerate.
3. Prepare relish plate the day before and cover well. Refrigerate.
4. Shape ice cream into balls ahead of time. Place in attractive serving dish. Return to freezer until needed.

Vivian's Beef Stroganoff

1 lb. ground beef
1 cup onion, chopped
1 clove garlic, minced
2 T flour
2 tsp. salt
¼ tsp. monosodium glutamate
¼ tsp. black pepper
¼ tsp. paprika

1 small can (3 oz. mushrooms and liquid
1 cup cream of chicken soup, undiluted
1 cup sour cream
snipped parsley for garnish

large package egg noodles

Brown together ground beef and chopped onion. When browned, add all other ingredients except sour cream and simmer uncovered about 10 minutes. Before serving, add sour cream to mixture. Simmer about 5 minutes. Serve in bed of noodles. Garnish with snipped parsley.

Marinated Green Bean Salad

1 can French cut green beans, drained
1 can yellow wax beans, drained
1 cup pickled beets, cut in strips
¼ cup bell pepper, minced
½ cup onion, minced

½ cup salad oil
½ cup vinegar
¾ cup sugar
1 tsp. salt
½ tsp. pepper

Combine all ingredients, toss, and refrigerate overnight.

White Mountain Relish Plate

In the center of your prettiest serving plate shape a mound of cottage cheese into which you have mixed 1 small, finely diced onion and enough parsley flakes to give color. Surround the cottage cheese with celery and carrot sticks. Add a few raw cauliflower florets.

23

Ice Cream

Ahead of time shape ice cream into balls with your ice cream scoop or large spoon. Place the balls in a large bowl and return to freezer. When serving, place each guest's ice cream dish on the table and pass the bowl of ice cream balls, letting him select his favorite flavor. Some of the pleasant advantages of serving ice cream in this way is that it avoids that last-minute struggle of scooping hard ice cream while family and guests wait for dessert. Also the ice cream bowl can be made very lovely with balls of raspberry or lime sherbet heaped together with vanilla ice cream.

HOW TO CONQUER PIE CRUSTS

There are two kinds of women in the world—those who say, "Pie crusts? Of course, just roll out the dough on a floured surface, place it in the pie pan, and flute the edge"—and those who roll out the dough on a floured surface, pry it loose, wrestle it into a pan, patch the holes, and then go out and buy a frozen pie.

My sympathy, empathy, and total identification is with this latter group. But I have discovered a wonderful plan, and now I can flute with the best of them. I want to share my plan with you.

First, see simple proportions and recipe listed below. Then, select a good, uneventful week when the long-range weather forecast does not prophesy any tornadoes and the children have not been exposed to the measles. Declare this to be "Pie Crust Week."

Each afternoon put on a fresh dress, make up your face and do whatever else helps you to get into a happy frame of mind and then go to the kitchen and make a pie. Use canned fillings or any simple recipe; do not try anything difficult. Remember your area of study this week is pie *crusts*, not pie fillings.

Do not skip a day making a pie. This is important because what you are really doing is training the eye and the hand to recognize the exact consistency and the characteristics of a good pie dough and even more, you are developing your confidence.

On Monday you will have your usual ragged and rather incredible pie crust. On Tuesday you will remember the consistency of the dough of yesterday and you will fearlessly add 1 tablespoon of water. Wednesday you will flour the board a bit more, and sticking will be a thing of the past. Thursday you will get the hang of rolling the dough from the center so that it keeps a more rounded shape and more even thickness. Friday you will try a new shortening. Saturday you will stand back and gasp in awe at this thing which you have wrought. And Sunday—Sunday you will hurry with the dinner dishes so you can rush down the block to talk with the neighbor women in the hope someone will mention the words "pie crust," and you can quickly say, "Pie crust? Of course. Just roll out the dough on a floured surface. . . ."

Pie Crust Recipe

Type	All-Purpose Flour	Shortening	Salt	Liquid
single shell	1 cup	⅓ cup	¾ tsp.	2½ to 3 T
double crust	1½ cup	½ cup	1 tsp.	¼ cup

Measure flour and salt into bowl. Cut in shortening with a knife, 2 knives, or a pastry cutter until small balls are formed. (Girls, these won't be perfect balls—not like a bowl of English peas.) Add water and mix lightly with a fork until dough barely holds together. Form into a ball with your hands. Place on floured board and roll with floured rolling pin. Place in pan and prick the bottom evenly. Try fluting the edge, remembering always that this is a skill which must be learned. Even Chopin did not write a perfect polonaise the first time he picked up a pen.

For a single shell place in hot oven (450°) until golden brown. This will take 10 to 15 minutes.

For a two-crust pie, line pie pan with pastry, pour in uncooked filling, cover with a top crust which has been pricked, and bake as directed for individual pie filling. (This will vary from pie to pie.)

Some If's Concerning Pie Shells and Crusts

1. If your dough sticks to the board upon which you are rolling it, there is just one answer—more flour.

2. If you are looking for the most convenient tools for rolling your crusts, try a pastry cloth and rolling pin cover and rub flour into both as directed. (The set costs about $1.00.)

3. If your fluting melts away and you lose your pretty pattern as the crust cooks, your dough has too much shortening.

4. If you have trouble holding a round circle as you roll the dough, remember always to roll out from the center.

5. If you are seeking a way to hold your pie crust in place firmly, practically hook each flute over the edge of the pan. This will prevent its falling back into the pan as it bakes.

6. If your shells creep down during baking, it may be because they are rolled too thin, are of uneven thickness, or have not been hooked over the edge of the pan.

7. If you have trouble cutting your rolled pie dough the right size for your pan, lay your pie pan upside down on your dough and cut around it with your spatula 1¼ inches out from the edge of the pan. Or, you may wait and trim off excess dough after placing the crust in the pan.

8. If you have not been pricking the unbaked dough, do start. This pricking lets trapped air escape from under a shell and allows steam to escape from a double-crust pie.

9. If you wish a browner crust at a lower temperature, try milk in your recipe instead of water.

10. If you wish to become an expert in this field, study the areas of "Flaky Pastry" and "Puff Paste" in other cookbooks. The basic principle of these two is dotting the rolled dough with shortening, folding over to make several layers, chilling, and rolling again.

⇥❧ MENU ❧⇤

7

A "Happy Mama Picnic" is one from which Mama returns with no messy baskets to unpack, no dirty dishes to wash, and no crumpled linen to handle. Such a picnic is ideal for a Sunday noon. Go by home after church and change into picnic clothes, take the food in its cartons from the refrigerator—and you are on your way.

The secret of such a picnic lies in a philosophy which can best be summarized as "relax and enjoy." It also is found in some simple mechanics of preparation.

One of these might be that of placing the food in disposable carriers. If your children enjoy do-it-yourself projects, your equipment might include serving bowls made from round, half-gallon ice cream cartons covered with shelf paper and decorated with cut out flowers. Or, you might find yourself with place mats made from brown paper bags which have a lazy daisy of looped yarn in the corner. Such projects will put you hours ahead in time saved and enjoyed.

For serving the following meal, you will need paper plates, napkins, and spoons. Take a knife for cutting watermelon.

Menu

Cold Fried Chicken Pieces
Ham Chunks, Pickles, and Olives
Individual Servings of Potato Salad
Bread and Butter Finger Sandwiches
Hard-boiled eggs
Lemonade
Watermelon Slices

Fix-Ahead Instructions

Prepare all foods ahead and wrap as designated. Refrigerate.

Cold Fried Chicken Pieces

Ahead of time fry chicken and allow to cool. Roll each piece
in a wrap of waxed paper. If the children are at work on this
project, let them gift wrap each piece by tying a bit of colored
yarn around the twisted end of the package.

Ham Chunks, Pickles, and Olives

Carry the ham chunks, pickles, and olives, which have been
well drained, to the picnic site in separate plastic bags. Combine all three in a round, half-gallon ice cream carton decorated with pictures cut from magazines. Place toothpicks close
by for spearing.

Potato Salad

5 medium potatoes
1½ cups celery, sliced
1 small onion, diced
2 T sweet pickle relish

1 T chopped parsley
1 tsp. salt
½ tsp. paprika
mayonnaise to moisten

Cook potatoes in jackets and allow to cool. Remove jackets
and cut potatoes into bite-sized cubes. Combine all other ingredients in a separate bowl and mix well. Pour over potatoes
and mix gently until potato pieces are coated. Place individual servings in paper cups. Set cups in box in refrigerator and
cover with waxed paper or foil.

Bread and Butter Finger Sandwiches

Spread slices of brown bread with butter and use white bread for top slices. Cut sandwiches in 4 narrow strips, making 4 finger sandwiches of one full-sized sandwich.

Boiled Eggs (wearing a hat)

hard-boiled eggs, 1 per person
cheese slices
stuffed olives

Hard-boil eggs. Cool and hull. With toothpick attach a 1-inch square of cheese to top. On top of cheese place a stuffed olive. Although it may not be too apparent to the grown-ups, the children will recognize this as a hat on their egg. For carrying, return to egg carton in paper bake cup.

Watermelon

If you usually cut the watermelons lengthwise, cut them around this time, or vice versa. Why? Gracious, I don't know, except that anything a little different makes the event a real occasion for a child. Besides, there are those about who insist they can tell what part of the country you were born in and something about your family background by the way you slice a watermelon. It's worth it just to mix them up a bit!

Lemonade

Prepare lemonade ahead and pour into thermos bottle or jug.

⊰⊱❃ MENU ❃⊰⊱

8

You may think this rice ring is difficult and tricky if you are not an old hand in the rice ring field, but do try it and discover how simple it really is. I have frozen it, allowed it to thaw, and then warmed it in the oven. I have also kept it in the refrigerator for as long as 3 days and then warmed it in the oven. It is foolproof, and it is very showy as well as good.

Menu

Rice Ring with Saucy
  Chicken
Grape Pineapple Salad
Asparagus with Pimiento
Cocoa Brownies with Ice
  Cream

Rolls and Butter
Coffee, Tea, or Milk

Fix-Ahead Instructions

1. Prepare rice ring and refrigerate.
2. Prepare chicken.
3. Prepare salad but do not add mayonnaise until ready to serve.
4. Bake brownies.

Rice Ring with Saucy Chicken

Rice Ring

2 cups uncooked rice
¼ cup parsley, chopped
¼ cup bell pepper, chopped
salt to taste

Take a large piece of waxed paper and fit it into your ring mold. Leave the ends of paper to extend up above the top of the mold for ease in handling. Cook rice and add seasonings. Pack the warm rice into the mold and allow to cool. Refrigerate. When cold, unmold on oven-proof dish by turning the mold upside down. The rice will come out immediately in a perfect mold because of the layer of waxed paper. Remove paper. Before serving allow to come to room temperature. Place in 350° oven for 10 to 15 minutes to heat through. Fill mold with chicken.

Saucy Chicken

2 T margarine
1 onion, chopped
1 can (3 oz.) mushrooms, drained
2 ribs celery, sliced
1 tsp. monosodium glutamate

1 tsp. Worcestershire sauce
1 can (2 cups) tomatoes
2 cups cooked chicken, diced
1 T cornstarch

Sauté onion in margarine. Add mushrooms and celery and continue to sauté. Add seasonings and tomatoes and simmer about 10 minutes. Add chicken. Mix cornstarch with 1 tablespoon water and add. Cook until slightly thickened. Spoon into rice ring and serve.

Grape Pineapple Salad

1 can pineapple bits, drained
2 cups seedless grapes
mayonnaise to moisten

Combine ingredients and mix.

Asparagus with Pimiento

Cook frozen or canned asparagus according to directions. Drain. Place in serving bowl and add ½ small jar pimiento, drained and cut in strips.

Cocoa Brownies Served with Ice Cream

1 cup margarine	5 T cocoa
2 cups sugar	1 tsp. vanilla
4 eggs	1 cup nuts
1½ cups flour	

Cream margarine and sugar. Add eggs and mix. Add flour and cocoa and mix. Add vanilla and blend before adding nuts. Put into greased pan and cook about 30 minutes at 350°. Serve with vanilla ice cream. These are light, cake-like brownies with a very delicate chocolate taste.

─═❋ MENU ❋═─

9

When the first nip of fall is in the air, remember warm casseroles with a hint of chili flavor, apple cider, and hot gingerbread.

Menu

Spanish Spaghetti   Crusty Bread and Butter
Apple Cider Salad   Coffee, Tea, or Milk
Refrigerator Gingerbread

Fix-Ahead Instructions

1. Prepare sauce for spaghetti.
2. Prepare salad. Place in mold. Refrigerate.
3. Mix ingredients for "Refrigerator Gingerbread" and refrigerate. Do not bake until just before serving.

Spanish Spaghetti

¼ cup vegetable oil   2 cups canned tomatoes
1 medium onion,   1½ cups American cheese,
  chopped   grated
½ tsp. salt   ¼ cup black olives, chopped
1 T chili powder   1 box (1 lb.) spaghetti

Place oil in pan and add chopped onion. Sauté until browned. Add salt, chili powder, and tomatoes. Mix well and simmer

34

about 20 minutes. Just before serving, cook spaghetti as directed on package. Pour sauce over drained spaghetti in greased casserole. Sprinkle with cheese and black olives. Bake at 350° long enough to melt cheese.

Apple Cider Salad

1 large pkg. apple gelatin
2 cups apple juice or cider, boiling
1 cup apples, chopped
½ cup celery, chopped
½ cup nuts, chopped

Prepare gelatin as directed on package, using hot apple juice rather than water to dissolve gelatin. Add other ingredients and pour into mold. Refrigerate.

Refrigerator Gingerbread

This recipe requires sour milk, which you may not always have on hand. You may substitute buttermilk or make your own sour milk by adding ½ tablespoon vinegar or lemon juice to ½ cup sweet milk.

½ cup shortening	1½ tsp. baking powder
½ cup sugar	½ tsp. soda
½ cup sour milk	½ tsp. salt
2 eggs	1 tsp. ginger
½ cup molasses	1 tsp. cinnamon
2 cups flour	1 tsp. allspice

Cream shortening, sugar, and 2 tablespoons sour milk. Add eggs and mix well. Add molasses. Sift all dry ingredients together twice. Add sifted ingredients alternately with remainder of sour milk to creamed mixture. Pour in greased, floured pan. Place in refrigerator until ready to bake and serve hot. Bake at 350° for 30 minutes. Cut in squares. Serve with whipped cream if desired.

❧❀ MENU ❀❧

10

A meal for teen-agers should not only be more than adequate, it should appear at first glance to be abundant, piled up, and running over.

Menu

Chili with Beans over Fritos   Soft Drinks
(served in individual Frito
sacks)
Fruit-and-Whatever Tray
Spreads with Crackers
Do-It-Yourself Sundaes

Fix-Ahead Instructions

1. Prepare chili bean mixture.
2. Prepare fruits, vegetables, or relishes for tray. Cover and refrigerate.
3. Prepare spreads for tray.
4. Cut ice cream into serving size cubes. Return to freezer.

Chili with Beans over Fritos

pot of chili with beans
Fritos, small sacks
onions, finely chopped
cheese, grated (optional)

On buffet or serving table place individual sacks of Fritos which have been slit down the side, not across the top, and a large pot of chili with beans. (Use canned chili and add beans, or use home-made chili recipe below.)

You will need 1 individual sack of Fritos for each girl, and I am embarrassed to report that if *my* boys are present, you may need as many as 3 for each boy.

Let each young person assemble his own meal by spooning the hot chili bean mixture over the Fritos which are still in their sacks. The sacks will be used as serving bowls. They will not be filled with chili, but rather the chili mixture will be used as dressing for the Fritos. My boys assure me that this should be done in just this way and that much is lost if the Fritos are served from one large bowl rather than from individual sacks. Allow the young people to sprinkle chopped onions over the chili in sacks and add a pinch of grated cheese.

Homemade Chili

Chili recipes vary all the way from this very basic one to those which include onions, green peppers, tomato paste, and so on.

1 lb. ground beef	2 to 4 T chili powder
2 to 3 T shortening	4 cups hot water
2 tsp. salt	2 cups cooked chili beans

Melt shortening in skillet. Add beef and brown. Add onions here if you like. Add salt, chili powder, and water. Cook slowly for 1 hour, stirring occasionally. Add beans.

While you are experimenting with chili, do try canned chili beef soup, using only half the amount of water suggested.

Spreads with Crackers

saltines
peanut butter
pimiento cheese spread

In the center of a large tray place two bowls. Fill one bowl with peanut butter. Fill the other with pimiento cheese spread. Surround the bowls with crackers. Place a few knives on tray for spreading.

Fruit-and-Whatever Tray

Use any fruits, vegetables, or relishes available. Some suggestions follow.

canteloupe slices	tomato chunks
watermelon slices	celery sticks
small bunches of grapes	carrot sticks
quarters of apples	
ripe peaches	pickles of all kinds

Arrange on a large tray and let the young people select. Have a large supply of paper napkins available.

Do-It-Yourself Sundaes

The budget will undoubtedly dictate just how elaborate the supplies for the sundaes may be. Below are some suggestions for ingredients which can be set up on a serving table. Let each guest assemble his sundae in a paper cup or glass.

ice cream (vanilla, chocolate, strawberry)
chocolate syrup
fruit syrup, any flavor
marshmallow cream
chopped nuts
maraschino cherries
whipped cream product in pressure can

Ahead of time, cut ice cream into serving-size cubes. Place cubes loosely in plastic bags or large freezer carton and return to freezer. This will prevent much struggling with hard ice cream as the teen-agers prepare their sundaes. (It will also do wonders for your nervous system.) Place trash cans nearby for Frito sacks, napkins, and paper cups.

➳➵❊ MENU ❊➶➴

11

Happiness (for the housewife) is the unexpected opportunity to have old friends in for Sunday dinner—and the realization that there is a big casserole of "Lasagne" already prepared in the freezer.

Menu

Lasagne   Crusty Bread and Butter
Green Salad with Avocados   Coffee, Tea, or Milk
Sherbet Loaf

Fix-Ahead Instructions

1. Prepare lasagne ahead and freeze.

Making lasagne is not only a matter of preparing food but also of enjoying an experience, much like making the Christmas cake or baking the Thanksgiving turkey. All ingredients of this recipe can be found on your grocer's shelves. The meat sauce needs to be simmered 3 hours, so plan to make it on an unhurried day.

My neighbor keeps this dish frozen as her insurance for spur-of-the-moment dinners. If you like, you can freeze only the sauce and prepare the noodles and bake just before serving. Or do as Marian does: prepare, bake, and freeze it, then heat before serving.

2. Prepare vegetables for green salad. Combine just before serving.

3. Prepare "Sherbet Loaf" ahead and freeze.

Lasagne

Meat Sauce

1 large onion, chopped	1½ T salt
2 cloves garlic, chopped	2 tsp. sugar
½ cup salad oil	1 tsp. basil
2 lbs. ground beef	½ tsp. pepper
2 cans tomato paste	2 bay leaves
¼ cup water	2 pinches oregano
½ cup chopped celery	3 to 4 lbs. canned tomatoes
¼ cup parsley	

Sauté onion and garlic in salad oil. Add ground beef and brown. Add remaining ingredients and simmer slowly for 3 hours.

1 lb. Lasagne noodles, cooked as directed on box
1 T salad oil
1 lb. cottage cheese
2 pkgs. (8 oz. each) mozzarella cheese slices
½ cup Parmesan cheese

Oil casserole. Place in layers Lasagne noodles, meat sauce, cottage cheese, mozzarella cheese slices, and Parmesan cheese. Bake at 375° about 15 minutes. Allow to stand 10 minutes to set layers. Cut in squares to serve, spooning sauce from pan freely over squares.

Green Salad with Avocados

Prepare your favorite green salad, using lettuce, tomatoes, and whatever vegetables your family likes best. Add cubes of avocado. Use vinegar and oil or Italian dressing.

Sherbet Loaf

This is a loaf to make when you aren't rushed and feel like doing something just for fun.

1 pint orange sherbet
1 pint lime sherbet
1 pint raspberry sherbet

Slightly soften orange sherbet and press into tube pan. Return to freezer. Next, slightly soften lime sherbet and press into tube pan to form a layer on top of the orange sherbet. Return to freezer. Next, slightly soften raspberry sherbet and press into a layer on top of the lime sherbet. Return to freezer. When completely firm again, unmold on your prettiest plate. Take to table on serving plate and cut as you would an angel food cake.

➳➽❃ MENU ❃❧❬ ❬

12

Someone has defined eternity as a big ham and two people. If you get caught with such a ham, you might try this dinner.

Menu

Escalloped Ham with Mustard Sauce
Celery, for Crunch *
Cheesed Potato Chips
Buttered Brussel Sprouts
No-Bake Chocolate Icebox Cake

Rolls and Butter
Coffee, Tea, or Milk

Fix-Ahead Instructions

1. Prepare ham. Bake just before serving. Prepare mustard sauce.
2. Prepare cake and refrigerate.

Escalloped Ham with Mustard Sauce

Escalloped Ham

2 cups ham, chopped
4 hard-boiled eggs, finely chopped

* Janey says that a meal without crunch is like a party without fun—definitely lacking somewhere.

1 can mushroom soup
1¼ cups bread crumbs
pepper to taste

Combine all ingredients. Place in greased casserole. Bake about 20 minutes at 350°.

Mustard Sauce

1 egg yolk	salt and pepper to taste
¼ cup sugar	paprika, a dash
½ T dry mustard	¼ cup vinegar
½ T flour	¼ cup milk

Beat egg yolk with fork. Add ingredients as listed, mixing after each addition. Cook over medium heat, stirring constantly for about 5 minutes until thickened. Serve hot or cold with any ham dish.

Cheesed Potato Chips

Spread potato chips in shallow pan. Sprinkle generously with grated American cheese. Bake at 350° about 10 minutes or until cheese is melted. Serve hot.

Buttered Brussel Sprouts

Cook frozen brussel sprouts according to directions on package. Season with butter as desired.

No-Bake Chocolate Icebox Cake

2 sticks margarine	3 egg yolks, beaten
2 cups powdered sugar	3 egg whites, beaten
3 squares baking chocolate, melted	20 vanilla wafers
	1 cup nuts, chopped

Cream margarine and sugar (you need not sift sugar). Add chocolate and eggs. Set aside. Crumble wafers and add nuts. Put half of wafer-nut mixture in greased 7 by 9-inch pan. Pour in chocolate mixture. Sprinkle rest of wafer crumbs on top. Refrigerate at least 4 hours. Cut in thin slices to serve.

→⊱✸ MENU ✸⊰←

13

This Iron Skillet Dinner requires about 1 hour on top of the stove or in the oven. It can be cooked ahead and then heated or put in the oven with the timer set. Prepare the rest of the meal ahead.

Menu

German Iron Skillet Dinner
Accompaniment Tray
Quick Fruitcake

Crusty Bread and Butter
Coffee, Tea, or Milk

Fix-Ahead Instructions

1. Prepare and cook iron skillet dish ahead and heat before serving, or prepare ahead and place in oven with timer set for 1 hour.
2. Prepare accompaniments ahead.
3. Prepare fruitcake at least 1 week ahead to allow the full flavor to penetrate.

German Iron Skillet Dinner

2 T margarine
2 lbs. chuck roast, cut
  in cubes
1 can sauerkraut,
  with liquid
4 potatoes, cut in chunks

1 medium onion, chopped
2 tsp. salt
1 tsp. pepper
1 tsp. monosodium glutamate
1 can tomato soup, undiluted

44

Melt margarine in heavy skillet, preferably iron. Add cubed beef and brown for about 10 minutes. Remove beef from pan. Place all other ingredients in pan and mix very lightly. One good stir around the pan is all that is needed. Place the beef chunks on top. Bake at 350° for 1 hour, or cook on top of stove about 45 minutes. Serve in the skillet in which it was cooked.

Accompaniment Tray

cottage cheese
raisin applesauce
raw cauliflower florets

In three bowls which group nicely, or in a tray with three compartments, place the cottage cheese, raisin applesauce prepared as directed below, and the washed, separated cauliflower florets.

Raisin Applesauce

To 1 can applesauce add ½ cup raisins and ½ cup nuts. Mix.

Quick Fruitcake

1 pkg. spice cake mix
½ cup applesauce
4 eggs, unbeaten
2 cups seedless raisins

1 cup mixed candied fruit
1 cup nuts
½ cup flour

Disregard instructions on cake mix package. Place cake mix, applesauce, and eggs in large bowl. Beat until smooth and creamy. Mix fruits and nuts with ½ cup flour and add to cake mixture. Blend well. Bake in greased, floured tube pan at 275° for 1½ to 2 hours.

This cake can be baked at least one week ahead and allowed to stand wrapped in foil. If you want to use it for a Christmas gift, decorate the top with nuts and bits of candied cherry. Try this also as an applesauce nut cake, replacing raisins and candied fruit with nuts.

SUGGESTED CURES
FOR "HOSTESS HORRORS"

Just before you put your head down on the pillow Saturday night, you may decide that your carefully planned Sunday dinner is not nearly adequate, that your special guests will go away hungry. If so, you have what is known as the "hostess horrors." This condition is quite normal for us girls—just like deciding that our children will starve to death while away at camp, or that the train carrying them to Grandma's will jump the track, never to be heard of again.

In order to help you combat your fear of guests fainting from hunger at your table, I have prepared a list of dishes that can be assembled quickly. Of course, you won't really need them. Your meal is already more than adequate, but these recipes will be worth a million dollars to your peace of mind in the moment of crisis. These are dishes you can create by running to the grocery store just as the weary grocer is trying to lock the door after a long, busy day. If you are skilful you may be able to get your husband to run for you, which will add greatly to marital bliss. You may discover an entirely new facet to his personality as he returns from the store with pajama legs hanging out below his pant cuffs. You may hear him muttering, "She has known these guests were coming for three weeks and now, now at this hour on Saturday night I have to run all over town hunting a grocery store that's open." Ignore all this. Tomorrow when you set your lovely meal on the table he will be just as proud as you are, and he will feel a fatherly pride toward those items he purchased under such stress last night.

Nothing makes a hostess feel so much like she is serving a Roman banquet as white and purple grapes spilling over the sides of a compote or piled high in a glass bowl. This grape compote route is usually the one I follow and after many years of marriage, Charles comes in without comment, bearing a big sack of grapes when guests are on the way.

Try olives stuck on toothpicks and in turn stuck into an apple, making "olive balls." This is a marvelous outlet for nervous energy. I can stick an unimaginable number of olives on toothpicks and into apples while the guests are ringing the front doorbell. This activity also has a side benefit. There is bound to be one effusive friend among your guests who will behold your art and say, "How clever!" In this hour of panic such a word as "clever" will come like an accolade trumpeted from some marble tower and may give you sufficient confidence to cause you to return to normalcy.

Some hostesses feel a great compulsion to add breads to a meal which threatens to be inadequate. As the checkers are slamming the covers on the cash registers, you or your husband can grab wheat bread, rye bread, garlic rolls, French bread, Italian bread, raisin bread, and so on. The varieties will serve as a conversation piece at the table. Besides, as the children come in from school next week they will enjoy oven-warmed garlic bread with lots of butter, brown bread with peach preserves, and so on. The bread will also freeze nicely, so you won't waste a thing.

Place a mound of cottage cheese on a plate and surround it with hastily drained, canned green mint pears and canned red apple rings. This will have such a professional look that it will bolster you beautifully.

Consider any fruits or melons in season. Sliced honey dew melons and canteloupe, cut from the rind and piled generously in a large bowl will add a look of abundance to any meal.

Try adding a tray of cheeses with crackers and relishes for nibbling. This is especially sensible since the cheeses will make such excellent sandwiches for the children next week.

In fall and winter hastily fill bowls with nuts, placing a nut cracker nearby. Guests tend to feel relaxed and at home as they merrily crack and eat. Also, as Christmas approaches, fill small bowls with hard candies. If your guests feel faint from lack of food, they can always pop a peppermint into their mouths.

Make a bowl of tangerine roses by pulling tangerine peel in sections halfway down the fruit. Bend the piece of peel forward and tuck it inside itself. If you have done this with superhuman speed and time hangs on your hands, with your kitchen shears cut the half-removed peel sections into petal shapes instead of tucking them under.

Remove applesauce from the can and place in bowl in center of salad plate which you have edged with cheese strips. Sprinkle the applesauce with cinnamon.

If you are still having "hostess horrors" even as the guests drive up the lane, open a can of whole kernel corn (don't try cream corn because in your state you will probably scorch it) and add slices of black olives. I suggest corn because it heats quickly.

Drain a can of purple plums. Place one plum in the center of a circle of drained pineapple which has been placed on a leaf of lettuce. (Time permitting, replace the plum seed with a miniature marshmallow or pecan half). Arrange these individual salads in a circle on your silver tray. In the center of the tray place a bowl of prepared poppy seed dressing, or "Catherine's Dressing" (p. 105).

Shine a pile of red apples and place a knife near them so guests will know they are for eating as well as for seeing.

Another interesting solution to the dilemma is to add soup to your menu. On Saturday night, get on a chair and poke into the most remote corner of the cabinet to get the rice bowls you bought in Chinatown when you were on vacation fifteen years ago. Just as the guests begin to arrive, pour into these bowls little servings of hot soup with a few crackers on the saucer beneath them.

Any canned soups will do nicely. I like chicken broth with cream and a dash of curry powder. Or, try cream with seasoned instant potatoes, prepared as directed on the package, and mixed into the cream to just the right consistency with lots of parsley on top.

You might add toast rounds with Parmesan cheese sprinkled on top. This is good with mushroom soup. Or, add cocktail sausages to celery soup.

Serve any soup with croutons. You may either buy them or simply cut stale bread in small cubes and fry in hot deep fat until they are golden brown. Drain well and put a few in each bowl or cup of soup.

➤➤❈ MENU ❈◀◀

14

This is one of my favorite meals for a special occasion, perhaps when long-anticipated guests are coming or when it is time for some family celebration such as a birthday. There is enough Hawaiian flavor to warrant bringing out the straw place mats and serving the salad in a hollowed pineapple half.

Menu

Oven Chicken from the Islands
Orange 5-Cup Salad
Broiled Sweet Potato Slices
Green Beans in Bacon Bundles

Rolls
Tea, Coffee, or Milk
Cake

Fix-Ahead Instructions

1. Cook sauce for chicken.
2. Prepare salad day ahead and refrigerate.
3. Arrange sweet potatoes on dish that can be placed under broiler.
4. Arrange beans in bacon bundles in stove-to-table pan.
5. Bake cake.

Oven Chicken from the Islands

3 lbs. frying chicken pieces

Brown chicken in margarine and place in covered casserole with skin side up.

Sauce for Chicken

½ stick margarine
¼ cup brown sugar
2 T cornstarch
1 tsp. salt
¼ cup vinegar

½ tsp. Worcestershire
sauce
2 T chili sauce
½ cup catsup
1 can (2 cups) pineapple
pieces, drained with
juice reserved

Melt margarine in pan. Add brown sugar, cornstarch, seasonings, and pineapple juice drained from pineapple pieces. Cook over low heat, stirring constantly until thickened. Add pineapple pieces.

Sunday morning, spoon prepared sauce over chicken and bake covered for 1½ hours at 350° while you are preparing breakfast. Heat before serving. Or, place in oven, covered, with timer set to bake for 1½ hours.

Orange 5-Cup Salad

Several Christmases ago this recipe, with numerous variations, ran through the kitchens of America. It is so easy and delicious I think it will remain a favorite.

1 cup (11 oz. can) mandarin orange sections, drained
1 cup shredded coconut
1 cup miniature marshmallows
1 cup nuts
1 cup sour cream

Combine ingredients and allow to stand several hours or overnight before serving. This recipe may be varied by using drained fruit cocktail rather than mandarin orange sections.

Broiled Sweet Potato Slices

1 can (1 lb.) sweet potatoes
2 T margarine
2 T brown sugar
1 tsp. cinnamon

Slice canned sweet potatoes and place cut side up in casserole. Blend margarine, sugar, and cinnamon. Spread on potatoes. Place under medium heat in broiler just long enough to warm potatoes and melt sugar mixture.

Green Beans in Bacon Bundles

Drain can of whole green beans, reserving liquid. Arrange whole beans in bundles of 4 or 5 beans. Place strip of bacon cut in half around beans and with joined bacon side down, lay in pan which can also be used as serving dish. Pour over beans 1 tablespoon melted margarine to which has been added ½ teaspoon salt and about half the liquid from the can. Cook over low heat until beans are done.

Hawaiian Iced Cake

1 box white cake mix, prepared and baked as directed
1 cup crushed pineapple, drained
1 cup shredded coconut
¼ cup nuts, chopped

Prepare cake mix as directed, and bake. Combine pineapple, coconut, and nuts and toss lightly. Fluff loosely on cake. If you want a topping with a spreading consistency, add whipped cream to pineapple-coconut mixture to moisten.

❧ MENU ❧

15

Pork Chops with Rice
Lettuce Chunks with Russian
  Dressing
Seasoned Lima Beans
Snowflake Fruit with Custard
  Topping

Rolls and Butter
Coffee, Tea, or Milk

Fix-Ahead Instructions

1. Prepare pork chops and rice ahead. As you leave for church, place in the oven with timer set for one hour.
2. Prepare "Russian Dressing."
3. Prepare fruit and topping separately. Combine just before serving.

Pork Chops with Rice

1 cup uncooked rice
1 onion, sliced
2 T parsley, snipped
½ cup celery, sliced

2 cups tomato juice
1 cup water
4 or more pork chops

In deep pan or iron skillet place uncooked rice. Place onions, parsley, and celery on top of rice. Pour tomato juice and water over. Place pork chops on top of rice mixture and bake covered at 350° for 1 hour.

Lettuce Chunks with Russian Dressing

head of lettuce
1 cup mayonnaise
⅛ cup chili sauce
2 T bell pepper, chopped fine

Cut head of lettuce into about 8 chunks. Combine ingredients and mix. Spoon dressing over lettuce chunks.

Seasoned Lima Beans

Cook frozen lima beans as directed on package, or heat canned beans. Season to taste with salt, finely diced onion, and bacon drippings.

Snowflake Fruit with Custard Topping

Fruit Mixture

2 oranges, peeled and sectioned
1 cup grapes, seeded or seedless
2 bananas, sliced
1 apple, cut into pieces
½ cup flaked coconut

Combine fruit. (I prefer to wait and add bananas and apples just before serving. However, if you are sure you completely cover each piece with the dressing, you can combine earlier and you will have a minimum of darkening of the fruit.)

Custard Topping

⅛ box vanilla pudding
¼ cup cream

Prepare the whole box of pudding as directed and save half for another meal. Place the half to be used in a separate bowl and add cream, unwhipped. This will have a very thin consistency. Pour lightly over fruit. Garnish with a twist of lemon peel which has a maraschino cherry anchored in the center with a toothpick.

➤❧❊ MENU ❊❧◄

16

I find this a good menu for a ladies' luncheon. Try using any colored glass plates you may have inherited or picked up here and there. The colors in glass are each so pretty that they always blend perfectly. Aunt Effie's old pale pink dessert bowls look right at home on my pale blue glass plates. The pale green ones, when used to serve whipped cream desserts, are especially effective with a sparkling clear glass plate under them to hold a favorite cookie. I find the bagged grocery store sand tarts the nearest thing to home-baked cookies.

Menu

Canned Soup or Chilled To-
    mato Juice
Assorted Crackers
Chicken Salad with Spiced
    Grapes
Cool Lime Relish Mold
Kay's Butter Cake

Tea or Coffee

Fix-Ahead Instructions

1. Chill tomato juice.
2. Prepare chicken salad and refrigerate.
3. Prepare lime relish mold and refrigerate.
4. Bake butter cake.

Chicken Salad with Spiced Grapes

2 cups cooked chicken, diced
2 cups celery, diced
1 can spiced grapes, drained
  (if unavailable, use fresh seedless grapes)

salt and pepper to taste
mayonnaise to moisten
lettuce

Combine ingredients as given. Mix until ingredients are moistened with mayonnaise. Serve on lettuce.

Cool Lime Relish Mold

1 large pkg. lime gelatin
1 cup green cabbage, finely
  shredded
¼ cup bell pepper, finely
  chopped
⅓ cup pared cucumber,
  chopped

2 radishes, sliced
1 tsp. horseradish
½ tsp. salt
pinch of pepper

Prepare gelatin as directed on box. Add other ingredients and place in pan to be cut in squares or in your favorite mold, and refrigerate overnight.

Kay's Butter Cake (made with margarine)

Since I have known Kay Bruce she has been making butter cakes and serving them in her own home, bringing them to parties and picnics, and last year she brought me a beautifully decorated one at Christmas time. Her recipe is adaptable and foolproof. Add frosting if you like, but it really isn't needed.

2 sticks margarine
1¾ cups sugar
2 cups flour

5 eggs
1 tsp. vanilla
2 tsp. almond extract

Cream margarine and sugar. Add 2 cups flour. Add eggs one at a time, beating after each addition. Add vanilla and almond flavoring. Bake in tube pan 1 hour at 325°.

➼❈ MENU ❈⇻

17

The children's knowledge of how to prepare a simple meal can at times prevent wild disorder in a family schedule. Here is a meal any child who is old enough to be trusted in a kitchen can prepare.

I am sure you have in your file many far more exciting recipes for spaghetti sauce than this one. The only consideration here was to discover a satisfying menu and a set of recipes that could be handed to a child who is eager to help but simply does not know where to start. Perhaps the hour comes to all of us when hot spaghetti and meat balls served by a proud little cook spells the difference between tension and relaxation.

Menu

Simple Spaghetti and Meat Balls

Lettuce Chunks with Tomato Wedges

Chocolate Sauce over Ice Cream

Hot Buttered Bread

Milk

Simple Spaghetti and Meat Balls

1 lb. ground beef
2 cans tomato soup

1 soup can water
¼ cup catsup

Shape meat into balls about 1 inch in diameter. Place tomato soup and water in a large saucepan. Add catsup and stir. Cook over medium heat until mixture begins to boil. Place each meat ball in boiling mixture with a serving spoon so as not to burn yourself. Let cook slowly about 15 to 20 minutes. Take one meat ball out and test to see if the meat is cooked. Cook spaghetti according to directions on the package. Drain the water off the spaghetti after it is cooked. Pour the sauce and meat balls over the cooked spaghetti and serve.

Lettuce Chunks with Tomato Wedges

Tear ¼ head of lettuce into bite-sized pieces. Add to this tomatoes which have been cut into 8 pieces each. Serve in a big bowl. Place a bottle of prepared dressing nearby.

Hot Buttered Bread

loaf of white or brown bread or sliced French bread
butter or margarine

Carefully remove from the package as much of the bread as you will need for this meal. Allow 2 slices per person. Lay the bread on a piece of foil and spread the pieces of bread with butter or margarine, placing them one against the other just as they were in the loaf. Pull the sides of the foil up over the bread to form a wrapper. Place bread in wrapper in the oven which is set at 300°, and heat for about 10 minutes.

Chocolate Sauce for Ice Cream

2 T margarine
2 T cocoa
1¼ cup sugar
⅔ cup milk
1 tsp. vanilla

Combine all ingredients in a saucepan. Place over medium heat and let come to a boil, stirring frequently. Boil about 1 minute. Remove from heat, let cool, serve over ice cream.

➤❈ MENU ❈⬅

18

This is a meal with a "south-of-the-border" flavor, although some of the dishes definitely have an origin farther north.

Menu

On the Border Casserole
Guacamole Salad
South of the Border Beans
North of the Border Squares
   with Butterscotch Sauce

Crusty Rolls and Butter
Coffee, Tea, or Milk

Fix-Ahead Instructions

1. Prepare casserole. Heat before serving.
2. Prepare Mexican beans. Freeze if you like.
3. Prepare cake and butterscotch sauce. Do not pour sauce over cake until just before serving.

On the Border Casserole

4 cups canned or frozen cooked corn
1 cup tomato soup or tomato paste
1 stick margarine, separated into bits with a fork or knife
¼ cup seedless raisins
¼ cup ripe olives
1 doz. canned tamales

Combine and mix all ingredients except tamales. Cut each tamale into halves and add pieces to corn mixture. Mix lightly so as not to break the pieces. If mixture seems too dry, add more tomato soup or paste. Place in greased casserole and heat through at 350°.

Guacamole Salad

2 ripe avocados
  (if they feel soft they are
  ripe)
1 small onion, minced
1 tomato, minced very fine

2 tsp. lemon juice
salt and pepper to taste
lettuce

Did you know the name "avocado" developed from the Aztec word *ahuacatl*? Call one of the garden club girls and ask her how to sprout the avocado seed and grow a little tree.
Peel avocados and remove seeds. Mash avocado. Add other ingredients. Mix and serve on a bed of lettuce. Prepare this just before serving to prevent avocados from darkening.

Mexican Beans

1 lb. pinto beans, dry
1 medium onion, chopped
1 clove garlic, minced
1 tsp. salt

1 T prepared mustard
½ tsp. black pepper
¼ tsp. chili powder
1 cup canned tomatoes

Soak beans overnight. Drain, cover with fresh water. Add all other ingredients and cook until beans are soft. Pour off excess water, if any. Place beans in greased casserole and bake at 350° about 1 hour. Real Mexican beans should be just one step this side of bean mush.

North of the Border Squares with Butterscotch Sauce

Prepare yellow cake mix and bake as directed.

Butterscotch Sauce

1 T margarine
2¼ T sugar
¼ cup milk
1 cup butterscotch morsels

Combine ingredients in saucepan and set in pan of hot water over heat. Allow butterscotch mixture to melt and blend. Pour hot or cold over cake squares.

➤➤❈ MENU ❈◄◄

19

An epicure dining at Crewe,
Found quite a large mouse in his stew.
  Said the waiter, "Don't shout,
  And wave it about,
Or the rest will be wanting one, too!"

Application: We all like something different once in a while.

From time to time as friends have sent me some of the recipes which appear in this book, they have added notes which said, "You can serve this to the governor," "Save this one for royalty," or, "This one is for the pastor's family." I have these same sentiments about this lamb curry dinner. It is the specialty of our house. It is actually husband Charles' recipe which he has developed from combining several curry recipes from here and there. It can be cooked in large quantities and frozen in meal-sized amounts.

The remainder of the meal is rather special also but at the same time easy to prepare.

Menu

Charles' Lamb Curry over   Hot Rolls and Butter
  Rice   Coffee, Tea, or Milk
Broiled Bananas

Ginger Canteloupe Balls
Curry Accompaniments
Vanilla Ice Cream

Fix-Ahead Instructions

1. If you like, cook curry weeks ahead and freeze.
2. Prepare "Ginger Canteloupe Balls" several days ahead and refrigerate.

Charles' Lamb Curry over Rice

1 leg of lamb (5 or 6 lbs.)	1 T cayenne
⅓ stick margarine	¼ tsp. ground ginger
2 medium onions, chopped	⅛ tsp. thyme
5 fresh tomatoes, cut up	1 T salt
¼ cup lemon juice	2 T flour
¼ cup curry powder	¼ cup milk
2 cups dried apples	2 cups kidney beans, canned

Melt margarine in a large pot and sauté onions and apples for 5 or 6 minutes. Remove lamb from bone and cut in small chunks. Add lamb to onions and apples; brown. Add all other ingredients except kidney beans, flour, and milk. Cover with water and cook for 2 hours. After 2 hours, make a paste of the flour and milk and blend with some of the juice from the pot. Add to mixture. Add kidney beans. Heat. Serve over hot rice. (Use instant rice for quick preparation.)

Broiled Bananas

bananas, ½ per person
2 T margarine
2 T sugar
¼ tsp. cinnamon
1 T lemon juice

Slice bananas in half lengthwise. Place in greased pan which can go under broiler. Melt margarine and add other ingredients to make sauce. Pour this over the bananas, and place under broiler until lightly browned.

Ginger Canteloupe Balls

canteloupe balls or cubes
⅓ cup water
1 cup brown sugar
¼ lemon, sliced
1 tsp. ground ginger

Make syrup by combining all ingredients. Boil for 5 minutes. Add canteloupe balls to syrup while still hot and allow to stand. When cool pour into a glass jar and refrigerate. These are lovely served in a clear glass bowl. They become an amber color after standing.

Curry Accompaniments

You may want to serve one or two of these with your curry. Serve all of them if your husband just got a raise in salary.

chutney, canned or homemade
hard-boiled eggs, chopped
bell peppers, diced or cut in narrow rings
cooked bacon, crumbled
tomato wedges
avocado, sliced
sweet or sour pickles
currant or cranberry jelly
salted peanuts or almonds
grated coconut

Vanilla Ice Cream

Serve only a small scoop.

❧❈ MENU ❈❧

20

Hunger may be the best sauce, but it is happiness that adds the flavor that lingers long after the last guest has gone and the last dish has been washed and put away.

Menu

Chicken Vivian   Tea, Coffee, or Milk
Waldorf Mold   Frozen Lime Pie
English Peas with Onion
  Slices
Rolls and Butter

Fix-Ahead Instructions

1. Prepare "Chicken Vivian." Either set oven to bake one hour while you are away, or bake while you prepare breakfast, allow to come to room temperature while you are gone, and return to 350° oven for 10 minutes just before serving.
2. Prepare "Waldorf Mold" a day ahead and congeal.
3. Prepare pie days ahead and place in freezer.

Chicken Vivian

3 cups cooked rice   2 cups cooked chicken, cut
¼ cup stuffed olives, chopped   in large pieces
¼ cup pecans, broken   1 can mushroom soup
                                    1 cup chicken broth

Combine rice, olives, and pecans. Toss lightly. Place half of mixture in a greased 1½-quart casserole. Combine cut chicken and mushroom soup. Spoon half over rice. Add remaining rice mixture. Top with remaining chicken mixture. Add broth. Bake covered at 350° for 1 hour.

Waldorf Mold

1 small pkg. lemon gelatin
1 cup chopped apples, unpeeled
½ cup celery, chopped
½ cup California walnuts, broken
¼ tsp. salt

Prepare gelatin according to directions on box. Add other ingredients and refrigerate.

English Peas with Onions

To a can of English peas add 2 slices onion, breaking rings apart. Heat well. Before serving, drain liquid. Add 2 tablespoons margarine and toss gently.

Frozen Lime Pie

1 baked pie shell
  or graham cracker shell
3 eggs, separated
½ cup fresh lime juice
½ tsp. vanilla
6 T sugar

1 can (15 oz.) sweetened
  condensed milk
1 tsp. lime rind, grated
3 or 4 drops green food
  coloring

Beat egg yolks until thick. Beat in lime juice. Add milk and stir until thick. Tint pale green with coloring. Beat egg whites, gradually adding sugar until stiff and shiny. Fold into lime mixture and pile in prepared crust. Decorate top with graham cracker crumbs or leave plain. Freeze until firm, about 4 to 6 hours. Before serving, you need not thaw more than a few minutes, as it retains an ice cream-like consistency.

⇒⧉⁕ MENU ⁕⧉⇐

21

Time and again I have had a recipe sent to me that I wish I had known years earlier. This salad-meat dish is such a recipe. It is ideal for Saturday lunches as well as prepare-in-a-minute Sunday dinners. If you are feeling festive, serve it in a small punch bowl with the hard-boiled eggs arranged on top.

Menu

Chilled Tomato Juice
Virginia's One-Dish Meat and
    Slaw Salad
Corn on the Cob
Angel Food Cake with Straw-
    berry Preserve Filling

Brown Bread and Butter
Tea and Milk

Fix-Ahead Instructions

1. Chill tomato juice.
2. Prepare dessert.

Virginia's One-Dish Meat and Slaw Salad

red and green cabbage, shredded (about ½ head each)
2 medium tomatoes, cut in wedges
4 eggs, hard-boiled and sliced
¼ lb. American cheese, julienne strips
6 pieces luncheon meat, julienne strips

Combine all ingredients and toss lightly. Pour your favorite dressing over sparingly. (French is excellent with this dish.)

Corn on the Cob

In water to which 1 teaspoon salt has been added, boil fresh or frozen corn until done. (Cooking time varies from 3 to 15 minutes with freshness and state of maturity of corn. Over-boiling makes corn tough.) Butter lavishly.

Angel Food Cake with Strawberry Preserve Filling

ready-baked angel food cake
⅛ cup strawberry preserves
⅛ pint whipping cream

Using a sharp knife, slice prepared angel food cake length-wise into 2 layers. Spread strawberry preserves between the layers. Whip cream and spread top and sides of cake with whipped cream. Add a few strawberry bits to top for garnish.

➤❈ MENU ❈◄

22

Here is a meal to remember when you want to say to friends, "Come have dinner with us, and do bring all the children." The recipes as given are for 4 to 6, but none suffers from being doubled or tripled.

Menu

Fruited Meat Loaf

Green Salad with Sliced,
   Hard-boiled Eggs

Mashed Potatoes with Butter

Instant Doughnuts with
   Plenty of Milk

Rolls and Butter

Coffee, Tea, or Milk

Fix-Ahead Instructions

1. Bake meat loaf ahead, or set timer to bake 40 minutes while you are away. Do not add fruit around loaf or broil until just before serving.
2. Prepare salad ingredients, cover, and refrigerate.
3. If you prefer to serve non-instant potatoes, cook ahead and mash.

Fruited Meat Loaf

Meat Loaf

1 lb. ground beef	1 egg
1 medium onion, chopped	1 tsp. salt
1 cup uncooked oats	1 tsp. pepper
⅓ cup evaporated milk	1 tsp. monosodium glutamate

Combine all ingredients and mix well. Shape into loaf in greased casserole. Bake about 40 minutes at 350°.

Fruit Garnish for Meat Loaf

When meat loaf is baked, surround it with halves of canned peaches, cut side up. On each half place 1 teaspoon brown sugar, then sprinkle with cinnamon. Between peach halves place a half slice of pineapple. Place meat loaf with fruit under broiler until sugar mixture melts.

Green Salad with Sliced, Hard-boiled Eggs

1 head lettuce, torn in pieces
2 tomatoes, cut in wedges
2 ribs of celery, chopped
2 green onions, chopped
hard-boiled eggs, ½ per person

Combine salad ingredients and place sliced eggs on top. Use French dressing sparingly.

Mashed Potatoes

Use instant potatoes or non-instant as preferred. But if you have prepared potatoes ahead, they must be warmed. Try it this way: Place cold mashed potatoes in a heavy saucepan. Add about ½ cup milk. Heat slowly, stirring from time to time. When potatoes are hot, remove from fire and whip vigorously until light and fluffy. Add more milk and butter as needed. Dot with butter and a dash of paprika.

Instant Doughnuts

prepared, canned biscuits
sugar

Cooking these doughnuts is for fun as well as for eating, so let the children help. But observe safety rules carefully. Think through your placement of the hot oil so there is no possibility of accident. Check to be sure that the deep fryer cord cannot possibly be reached by a small hand. Do not leave the hot oil unattended for a moment.

Now that I have scared you to death, I will tell you how to make the doughnuts.

Place about 4 cups of oil in a deep container or deep fryer. Heat. With a cutter remove the centers from prepared, canned biscuits. Drop rings into the hot oil and allow to fry until nicely browned. Remove and drain on paper towels. Also fry the "holes" and add a dash of cinnamon.

Place in front of each child a piece of waxed paper on which you have spooned a little mound of sugar. The doughnuts should be rolled while still warm.

‑⊁✻ MENU ✻⊱‑

23

This is a meal for the day when the best-laid plans of Mother, along with those of "mice and men," have already "gang a-gley." If Saturday was too busy for more than bare minimum preparations, try this. Cook chicken ahead (or use canned chicken if things are this far a-gley). Prepare the remainder of the meal when you get in from church. Time? Less than 30 minutes.

Menu

Sandwich in a Casserole   Coffee, Tea, or Milk
Buttered Broccoli (see p.
  10)
Fresh Fruit
Hot Quick Cookies

Fix Ahead-Instructions
1. Cook chicken. Cool. Remove from bones in slices.

Sandwich in a Casserole
chicken slices
toast slices
1 can cream of chicken soup
¼ soup can heavy cream
sprinkling of Parmesan cheese

72

Place slices of toast in casserole. Cover with slices of chicken.
Over this pour cream of chicken soup which has been diluted
with ½ can heavy cream. Sprinkle with Parmesan cheese. Bake
at 350° about 10 minutes.

Fresh Fruit

grapes
apples
bananas
peaches

Arrange fruit in a large bowl. Place knives nearby for cutting
fruit.

Hot Quick Cookies

These cookies are so simple one of the children can make
them while you are putting the casserole together.

1 cup biscuit mix
1 box pudding mix (any flavor)
1 egg
¼ cup cooking oil

Combine ingredients and shape dough into balls the size of a
walnut. Place on cookie sheet. Flatten balls with your thumb
and place 1 chocolate chip in the center of each. Bake at 350°
about 8 minutes or until lightly browned. These may be used
as little party cookies because they are so uniform in size and
lend themselves to decorations.

⭐✖ MENU ✖⭐

24

The thought of company for dinner doesn't have to scare the *new bride*. Everyone fixes that first company meal sometime, and Sunday noon is as good a time as any. I was far from home and Mother when I prepared my first company dinner, and I asked a lady in the grocery store what I should fix. She suggested fried chicken with gravy and potatoes. Gravy? Really now! I still shudder before I attempt gravy for guests.

Menu

Cold Ham Slices with Pine-
    apple Rings
Peach Salad
Asparagus Casserole
Pound Cake with Plum Pre-
    serve Topping

Bread and Butter
Coffee, Tea, or Milk

Fix-Ahead Instructions

1. Prepare ham and pineapple tray the day before. Cover with foil and refrigerate.
2. Prepare peach salad. Cover with foil and refrigerate.
3. Combine all ingredients for asparagus casserole but do not bake. Refrigerate covered. Take out of refrigerator as you leave for church and allow to come to room temperature. Place

in oven when you return. Casserole will need about 15 minutes at 350°.

4. Buy cake ahead. Prepare topping but do not put on cake until ready to serve.

Cold Ham Slices with Pineapple Rings

canned ham
1 can pineapple slices, drained

Carefully read instructions on canned ham. Be sure it is pre-cooked and ready to eat. Slice ham and place it on tray or plate. Arrange pineapple slices artistically among the slices of ham. (Allow 2 medium slices of ham and 2 slices of pineapple for each guest.)

This dish is now ready to serve. Cover with foil and place in the refrigerator until you are ready to serve it.

Peach Salad

1 can peach halves, drained
½ 8-oz. pkg. cream cheese
  (save the other half for
  your dessert)

1 T milk
¼ cup broken nuts
head of lettuce

On a large plate place pieces of lettuce—fondly called lettuce cups since ideally they cup up at the edges—one for each guest. In each lettuce cup place a well-drained peach half with the cut side up. In the hollow of the peach place dressing.

Dressing

Leave cream cheese out of refrigerator until it comes to room temperature. To one half of the 8-ounce package of cheese add 1 tablespoon of milk and mash with a fork until creamy and smooth. Add ¼ cup broken nut meats.

Now, everyone *expected* you to have ham with peach salad, so let's dazzle them on this next dish. It is very simple and it is the only thing you will need to give a thought to before serving. The other dishes you will just take from the refrigerator and set on the table, which was completely set ahead of time.

Asparagus Casserole

1 can (2 cups) asparagus	2 hard-boiled eggs
1 can celery soup, undiluted	bread crumbs or cubes
¼ lb. American cheese (roughly the size of your compact)	

All preparation can be made ahead. Drain asparagus, reserving liquid. (This means save it because you're going to need it later. Well, never mind if you have already poured it down the sink. Just forget it and don't get excited. This is a good lesson in cooking: if one thing messes up, just try something else.) Place asparagus in oven-proof casserole.

Place one can of celery soup in small bowl and add juice from asparagus can. (If it is already down the drain and heading off for the Highland Park Disposal Plant, use 1 cup milk instead.) Cut cheese into tiny pieces or grate and add to this mixture. Pour over asparagus in casserole. Peel hard-boiled eggs (eggs placed in pan of cold water over medium heat and cooked for 12 minutes). Slice them, placing slices on top of mixture in casserole. Now cover the top with bread crumbs. (Take 2 slices of dry bread or toast and with a knife, cut them into cubes about ½ inch across. Or, if an electric blender was among your wedding gifts, break dry bread into it and turn it on.) Cover casserole with foil and refrigerate. Before you leave for church, remove casserole from refrigerator and allow to come to room temperature. When you return, bake at 350° for about 15 minutes and serve.

Pound Cake with Plum Preserve Topping

1 ready-baked pound cake, bought from the bakery department of your grocery store

Slice cake just before serving and add topping made in the following way:

Topping

½ 8-oz. pkg. cream cheese (the other half of the package you used for the salad dressing)

1 T milk
3 T plum preserves

Allow cream cheese to come to room temperature. Add milk and mash with fork until creamy. Add preserves and mix.

I discovered the joys of plum preserves once when I baked a spice cake which turned out like well-tanned leather. I had hailed 8 neighbors in from their yards, telling them that I had a cake just coming out of the oven. The thing I had on hand was plum preserves, so I fixed it just as I have told you and spread it on the dry cake very lavishly. Three women asked for the recipe. Now I sometimes run out of bread and milk, but plum preserves I have always on hand—good insurance.

❧❦ MENU ❦❧

25

It's time for dinner on the patio.
Lay the stuffed hamburgers on the grill. Bring the relishes from the refrigerator. Warm the beans and give the prepared biscuits a few minutes in the oven and you are ready. Bake the dessert while you are serving the hamburgers.

Menu

Stuffed Hamburgers   Onion Biscuits
Celery Sticks   Coffee, Tea, or Milk
Baked Beans with Pineapple
   Chunks
Quick Cobbler

Fix-Ahead Instructions

1. Prepare stuffed hamburgers. Do not broil until just before serving.
2. Prepare celery sticks. Refrigerate.
3. Prepare baked beans. Heat before serving.
4. Combine dry ingredients for cobbler. Add milk and stir just before pouring into casserole. Add fruit to casserole and bake.
5. Prepare spread for onion biscuits, but do not put on biscuits until ready to bake.

Stuffed Hamburgers

78

hamburger buns   ½ lb. American cheese, sliced
2 lbs. ground beef
salt and pepper to taste

Shape ground beef to which you have added salt and pepper into very thin patties. On top of 1 pattie place a 2-inch square of sliced cheese. On top of cheese place 1 tablespoon of dressing, described below. Place second thin pattie on top of dressing. Seal edges of two thin patties together by pressing edges. You are sealing the cheese and dressing between the two patties. Broil patties slowly until meat is done. The cheese inside will be melted with the dressing. Serve on heated hamburger bun.

Dressing

1 tsp. prepared mustard
1 small onion, chopped
1 T pickle relish (your family's favorite)
mayonnaise to make the proper consistency

Celery Sticks

Prepare celery sticks or other fresh relishes or crunchy vegetables.

Baked Beans with Pineapple Chunks

There is nothing simpler or more satisfying than the standard baked beans made with pork and beans. Here is a recipe, probably much like the one you use. Try adding pineapple chunks for a special touch.

1 medium onion, chopped   2 T molasses
2 T bell pepper, chopped   2 T brown sugar
2 T margarine   1 tsp. prepared mustard
1 can (2 cups) pork and   ½ cup pineapple chunks
   beans
½ cup catsup

Sauté the onion and green pepper in margarine. Add the other ingredients. Bake at 350° about 40 minutes, or if you are pressed for time, heat on top of stove and then place in the oven for 15 to 20 minutes.

Quick Cobbler

½ cup sugar
½ cup flour
½ cup milk
1 tsp. baking powder

¼ tsp. salt
2 cups sweetened fruit
(fresh, frozen, or
canned)

Mix all ingredients except fruit and pour into greased casserole. Add 2 cups sweetened fruit. Bake at 350° for 40 minutes. This is one of those magic recipes in which you begin with the crust on the bottom and end with it on top.

Onion Biscuits

prepared, canned biscuits
2 T margarine, melted
1 tsp. garlic salt
1 tsp. onion salt or finely diced onion

Melt margarine and add to it the garlic salt and onion. Brush top of prepared biscuits with butter mixture and bake as directed on package.

HOW TO MAKE MOLDS

There is nothing magical about molds. If they have frightened you away, try this system for preparation and unmolding.
1. For a very stiff mold use ⅛ less water than is directed on gelatin package instructions. Often as you add other ingredients such as fruit to your mold, you add liquid without being aware of it.
2. Grease mold lightly if you wish. For a salad mold, grease the mold with mayonnaise. Pour liquid gelatin mixture into mold.
3. Refrigerate.
4. When fully congealed, remove from refrigerator and set in pan of lukewarm, not hot, water while you count to 7 slowly (*only* 7).
5. Turn mold upside down on serving dish.
6. Be patient.
7. Let mold alone and let it ease out. There is not a recorded instance of a mold that never unmolded.
8. If you can't stand it, put a washcloth which has been wrung out in hot water over top of mold.
9. When you peek under and see that the salad or dessert is now on the plate, lift mold off and sigh with pleasure.
10. Return molded salad or dessert to refrigerator until time to serve.

❧❧❀ MENU ❀❧❧

26

Now, put into practice all you have learned on the preceding pages with this "Chicken and Mandarin Orange Mold." You will feel like a princess with a full staff of servants as you ride home from church to a completely prepared meal.

Menu

Chicken and Mandarin
  Orange Mold
Stuffed Eggs
English Pea Salad
Fudge Pie

Hot Rolls
Coffee, Tea, or Milk

Fix-Ahead Instructions

1. A day ahead prepare "Chicken and Mandarin Orange Mold."
2. Prepare stuffed eggs and cover tightly. Refrigerate.
3. Prepare English pea salad and refrigerate.
4. Bake fudge pie.

Chicken and Mandarin Orange Mold

1 large pkg. lemon gelatin
1 pkg. (3 oz.) cream cheese
2 cups cooked chicken, cubed
1 apple, diced

1 can mandarin orange
  sections, drained
½ cup black olives,
  sliced

Prepare lemon gelatin according to package directions, using ⅓ less water for stiff mold. Add room-temperature cream cheese and dissolve in warm gelatin. Cool slightly. Add other ingredients. Mix. Pour into mold. Refrigerate.

Stuffed Eggs

Hard-boil eggs. Cool. Cut in half lengthwise. Remove yolks and place in bowl. Mash with fork. Add salt and pepper to taste, 1 teaspoon sweet pickle relish, and enough mayonnaise to moisten. Return mixture to white section of eggs. Add dash of paprika.

English Pea Salad

2 cans English peas, drained
1 medium onion, finely chopped
½ cup chopped celery
½ cup American cheese, cut in ½-inch cubes
¼ cup sweet pickles, cut in pieces
salt and pepper to taste
¼ cup mayonnaise, to moisten

Drain peas. Add all other ingredients and mix. Refrigerate until time to serve. (Keeps several days covered and chilled.)

Fudge Pie

2 squares bitter chocolate
½ cup margarine
1 cup sugar
4 T flour
2 eggs
1 teaspoon vanilla

½ cup chopped pecans
pinch of salt

Melt chocolate and margarine in double boiler. In separate bowl beat eggs slightly, add sugar, flour, vanilla, salt, and pecans. Pour mixtures together and blend. Bake in 9 inch pie pan at 350° for 30 minutes. Serve warm with or without vanilla ice cream.

➤❈ MENU ❈◄

27

Since bell (green) peppers are called for in so many recipes, it is a delight to have them always on hand. Try growing a plant or so in the backyard among the flowers. The plants themselves, with their dark glossy leaves, are as ornamental as shrubs, and it is a pleasant experience to harvest enough of your own peppers to serve this meal. We have 5 plants this year, and we have given peppers to neighbors, chopped and frozen them in half-cup packages, and the bushes are still loaded.

Menu

Green Peppers Filled with
   Tuna Salad
Easy Lime Mold
Mildred's Stuffed Yellow
   Summer Squash
Brim's Quick Cherry Dessert

Bread and Butter
Coffee, Tea, or Milk

Fix-Ahead Instructions

1. Prepare tuna salad. Cook peppers just before serving.
2. Prepare lime mold and refrigerate.
3. Prepare stuffed summer squash and have ready to slip into oven for heating.
4. Prepare cherry dessert and bake and serve cold. Or, pre-

pare ahead and bake while the family is eating the main course, and serve hot.

Bell Peppers Filled with Tuna Salad

Bell Peppers

Cut tops from peppers. Remove seeds and membrane with spoon, preferably a grapefruit spoon. Boil in hot water for 6 to 10 minutes.

Tuna Salad

2 small cans tuna	salt and pepper to taste
2 eggs, hard-boiled	mayonnaise to moisten
1 medium tomato, chopped	pickles, chopped (optional)

Combine ingredients listed above. Place salad in prepared peppers.

Easy Lime Mold

1 small pkg. lime gelatin
1 pkg. (3 oz.) cream cheese
1 can (2 cups) fruit cocktail, drained

For convenience, in your mixer bowl prepare gelatin according to directions on package. While liquid is still warm, add cream cheese which has been cut in pieces. Blend thoroughly with mixer and add drained fruit cocktail. Pour into mold and refrigerate.

Mildred's Stuffed Yellow Summer Squash

yellow summer squash, 2 per person
2 T margarine
1 small onion, finely minced
½ tsp. salt
1 wiener, cut very fine, *or*

3 slices bacon, cooked and crumbled

Boil squash whole until tender. Test with fork for tenderness. Drain and allow to cool. Cut one side from squash and remove centers and seeds, reserving all to make stuffing. The squash will look like little yellow boats. Place squash boats side by side in greased casserole. Mash all reserved squash. Add margarine, finely chopped onion, and finely chopped wiener. Add salt to taste. Return this mixture to the squash boats in casserole. Heat well before serving. I like to serve these because they are as pretty as they are tasty. They can be prepared and kept overnight in the refrigerator before heating and serving.

Brim's Quick Cherry Dessert

1 can sour cherries (do not drain)
½ cup sugar
1 pkg. butter pecan coffee cake mix (ignore directions for use)
1 stick margarine, melted

Put cherries in greased baking dish. Sprinkle sugar over. Sprinkle coffee cake mix over top. Pour melted margarine over and bake at 350° for 30 minutes. Serve hot or cold. If the mix which you bought has a topping mix with it, prepare this mix as directed and add to top after dessert is cooked. Milk, cream, whipped or ice cream also add a great deal to this dessert.

➤➤✦ MENU ✦◄◄

28

From time to time it seems to happen. Saturday night arrives and not only is the cupboard bare but also the oven and the deepfreeze. There is just time for a quick trip to the drive-in grocery to pick up supplies for Sunday dinner. This is a meal for such an occasion—straight from the grocer's shelves, but with some home-cooked touches added.

Menu

Beef Pie with Biscuit Top-
  ping
Spinach with Tiny Boiled
  Onions
Cottage Cheese Variety Salad
Cherry Fool

Bread and Butter
Tea and Milk

Beef Pie with Biscuit Topping

2 cans (1½ lbs. each) of prepared beef stew
2 large onions
2 pkgs. prepared, canned biscuits

Place prepared stew in serving pan which can be used both on top of stove and in the oven. Add sliced onion to stew and simmer 10 minutes. Place biscuits on top of hot stew and place in oven. Cook as directed on biscuit package. (Be sure the stew is thoroughly heated before placing the biscuits on top, or the biscuits will not cook properly on the bottom.)

Spinach with Tiny Boiled Onions

1 can spinach
1 can boiled onions

Add can of tiny boiled onions to can of spinach and heat through. Season with salt and butter.

Cottage Cheese Variety Salad

1 pint cottage cheese
1 can fruit cocktail, drained
¼ cup nuts

To one pint of cottage cheese add 1 can of drained fruit cocktail and ¼ cup nuts.

Cherry Fool

1 pint whipping cream
1 can prepared cherry pie filling

Whip cream and fold in cherry pie filling. Serve in individual dessert dishes.

➤➤✸ MENU ✸◄◄

29

A Spanish proverb says that four persons are necessary to make a good salad: "A spendthrift, for oil; a miser, for vinegar; a barrister, for salt; and a madman, to stir it up."
Visualize three spendthrifts and one miser and you have the correct proportions for oil and vinegar dressing. Add a dash of barrister and let the madman go wild on the salad below.

Menu

Giant Shrimp, Cheese, Vege-
    table Salad
Carousel Corn
Chocolate Peppermint Pie

A Variety of Crackers
Coffee, Tea, or Milk

Fix-Ahead Instructions

1. Prepare all ingredients for salad. Do not combine until just before serving.
2. Prepare corn and refrigerate.
3. Bake pie.

Giant Shrimp, Cheese, Vegetable Salad

2 lbs. frozen shrimp, boiled as directed on pkg.
½ lb. American cheese, cut in ¼-inch cubes
1 head lettuce

4 tomatoes
1 cucumber, thinly sliced
¼ cup radishes, thinly sliced
1 cup celery, diced
1 cup pickled pearl onions, drained
1 can green beans, chilled, drained (optional)
1 can asparagus tips, cooked, chilled, drained (optional)

Combine ingredients. Serve with a choice of salad dressings and a variety of crackers.

Corn Carousel

1 can whole kernel corn, drained	salt
1 small onion, finely chopped	pepper
1 bell pepper, finely chopped	cayenne
French dressing or mayonnaise, to moisten	paprika

Combine corn, onion, and pepper. To dressing add seasonings and mix well. Add to corn mixture and stir. Serve hot or cold but do serve in a clear crystal or a green bowl.

Chocolate Peppermint Pie

1 baked pie shell

1 box chocolate pudding-and-pie filling
½ pint whipping cream
few drops of peppermint extract *or* finely chipped peppermint candy

Prepare boxed pudding as directed. Cool slightly and pour into prepared shell. Top with whipped cream to which you have added the peppermint extract or chipped peppermint candy.

➤➤➤ MENU ➤➤➤

30

This meal is for "Adults Only," not because it would not be good for the children, but rather it is not a meal that would appeal to most children. It is ideal for that Sunday when the children are away at camp or when the teen-agers are set up for hamburgers on the patio and the adults go into the dining room with the air-conditioner.

Menu

Simple Crab Mornay on
  Toast Strips
Carrot Curls, Celery Fans,
  and Olives
Buttered Asparagus
Nancy's Chocolate Almond
  Pie

Hot Rolls and Butter
Coffee, Tea, or Milk

Fix-Ahead Instructions

1. Combine ingredients for crab Mornay as directed, but do not add cheese and crab meat until ready to heat and serve.
2. Prepare carrot curls and celery fans.
3. Bake pie.

Simple Crab Mornay on Toast Strips

1 stick margarine
5 green onions, finely chopped
2 T flour
1 pint cream *or*
   1 can (13 oz.) evaporated milk plus ¼ cup sweet milk
¼ cup snipped parsley
½ tsp. salt
¼ tsp. nutmeg
½ tsp. pepper
few drops Worcestershire sauce
1 lb. cooked crab meat (canned or frozen)
½ lb. Swiss cheese, grated

In heavy pan sauté onions in margarine. Add flour and blend. Add cream and seasoning to taste. Add crab and grated cheese and simmer until cheese is melted and bubbly. Serve over toast cut in strips or in pattie shells. This is also good as a warm dip for your Christmas open house. It freezes well if you would like to fix it far ahead.

Carrot Curls, Celery Fans, and Olives

Carrot Curls

Scrape carrots. Lay carrot on cutting board and with a vegetable peeler or floating knife press down and shave off thin carrot layers. Wind carrot layers around finger and put them in ice water in wide-mouthed jar.

Celery Fans

Cut celery ribs into 4-inch lengths. With knife make a number of cuts from large end to within 1 inch of other end. Place in ice water in wide-mouthed jar.

Olives

Place an assortment of black, green, and stuffed olives on dish with carrots and celery.

Buttered Asparagus

Prepare frozen asparagus as directed on package, using butter and lemon to season.

Nancy's Chocolate Almond Pie

1 stick margarine

¾ cup sugar

1 square (1 oz.) baking chocolate, melted

1 tsp. vanilla

2 chilled eggs

½ pint whipping cream

2 T sugar

1 tsp. vanilla

1 baked pie shell

Cream together margarine and sugar. Melt chocolate in pan over hot water and add to sugar mixture. Add vanilla and chilled eggs, beating 2 minutes after each egg. Pour into baked pie shell. Before serving, top with sweetened whipped cream with vanilla added. Sprinkle whipped cream with almond slices that have been browned in 1 tablespoon margarine. Stir almonds constantly while browning.

❧❧❦ MENU ❦❧❧

31

This is a Sunday dinner for a hot summer day when all the children will be present—and hungry. This "Wieners in a Cloud" recipe needs to be in the oven only long enough to bake the prepared canned biscuits.

Menu

Wieners in a Cloud   Bread and Butter
Baked Beans   Iced Tea and Milk
Bacon Potato Salad
Congo Squares
Strawberry Punch

Fix-Ahead Instructions

1. Prepare beans. Before serving, heat thoroughly with garnish on top.
2. Prepare potato salad a day ahead. Refrigerate.
3. Strawberry punch can be prepared ahead. Add ginger ale just before serving.
4. Prepare "Congo Squares" a day ahead, or prepare weeks ahead and freeze.

Wieners in a Cloud

Wieners, 2 or 3 per person
Canned biscuits (same number as wieners)

Fold unbaked biscuits around uncooked wieners and pinch biscuit sides together to form circle around center of wiener. Place on cookie sheet side by side and bake according to directions for cooking biscuits. When you remove these from the oven you will have a juicy cooked wiener surrounded by a collar of fluffy browned biscuit. Have catsup available.

Baked Beans

2 cans (1 lb. each) baked
    beans
2 cloves garlic
2 T brown sugar
½ cup chili sauce

For Garnish:
2 large onions
2 large tomatoes

Combine beans, garlic, brown sugar, and chili sauce. Cook over low fire about 30 minutes. Before serving, pour into shallow baking dish. Alternate a slice of tomato and a slice of onion around the sides of the dish on top of beans. Place in oven and bake about 15 minutes. This can share the oven with your "Wieners in a Cloud."

Bacon Potato Salad with a Crunch

6 to 8 medium potatoes
½ cup onion, chopped
1 cup celery, chopped
3 hard-boiled eggs, chopped
⅓ cup crisp bacon, crumbled

2 T bacon drippings
¼ tsp. pepper
1 tsp. salt
mayonnaise to moisten

Boil potatoes in skins until done. (Test with a fork.) Cool. Remove skins and cut potatoes into cubes. In separate bowl combine all other ingredients. Add to potatoes and toss gently until potatoes are coated with dressing. Allow to stand several hours or overnight before serving.

Strawberry Punch

1 small pkg. strawberry gelatin
4 cups hot water

1 can (6 oz.) frozen lemonade, diluted as directed
¼ cup sugar
1 large bottle ginger ale

Add to package of gelatin 4 cups hot water. Stir. Allow to cool. Add diluted lemonade and sugar. Before serving add ginger ale. This makes about 12 large glasses. Don't fret about the gelatin's starting to congeal. It wouldn't dare with so much additional liquid.

Congo Squares

⅔ cup shortening
1 pkg. (1 lb.) brown sugar
  (about 2¼ cups)
2¾ cups sifted flour
2½ tsp. baking powder

½ tsp. salt
3 eggs
1 pkg. chocolate bits
1 cup nuts or raisins

Melt shortening. Add brown sugar and blend. Add dry ingredients and eggs and beat well. Add nuts or raisins and chocolate bits. Pour into greased pan 9 by 13 inches. Bake at 350° for 30 minutes. Cut in squares when cool. Yield: about 4 dozen.

SOME THOUGHTS
ON COOKING ROASTS

While working on this book, I have talked and corresponded with dozens of homemakers all over the country. I have asked them, "What do you most frequently fix for Sunday dinner after church?" Again and again they have said "beef roast" or "pot roast." As we have talked further, I have found that each cook has her own system of preparation. She has worked out small variations here and there in accordance with the likes and dislikes of her family and also in accordance with her own cooking facilities. One of the delightful and amazing things about this individual art of cooking is that often while one good cook reported one method of preparation, another equally good cook immediately said, "Oh, I would never do that."

Here are some of the methods of preparation mentioned to me, along with some general information concerning cooking meats. You will have to be the judge of the system you like best.

Cold sliced beef, cooked ahead and served with hot soup and cold salads, seemed to be a favorite. Roast beef sandwiches served with a green salad and lots of ice cream was announced as a winner for summer Sundays. Roast beef with mashed potatoes and gravy—delicious, everyone agreed. However, most added that they did not serve this as often as other menus because of the expanding waistline problem.

Caroline has worked out an excellent system for roast leg of lamb with potatoes, her Sunday dinner specialty. She prepares a 5-to-6-pound roast by rubbing it with thyme. She sets the oven at 300° and plans to cook the roast 30 to 35 minutes per pound. As she leaves the house at 9:30 she turns the oven on, letting the meat cook while she is away.

One mother told me that she often divides an inexpensive cut of roast into chunks and places it in a heavy pan in the oven with an abundance of prepared bar-b-que sauce spread over. This system greatly cuts down on the cooking time required.

Another good cook reported that she sometimes cooks a roast on Saturday. When it has cooled, she slices it and places the slices in a casserole. On Sunday before serving it, she pours heated onion, tomato, or mushroom soup over and heats through.

Joyce said that she works with frozen prepared vegetables for a pot roast. For her time schedule this is by far the best. In fact, she reports that all is not lost if she forgets to take the roast from the freezer the night before. She simply places it in a 400° oven while she prepares breakfast. Then, before leaving for church she adds fresh onions, frozen carrots, frozen potatoes, and seasonings for the vegetables and reduces the oven temperature to 300°. A big hot meal is ready as the family comes in from church.

Ahead of time she has prepared potatoes by peeling and cutting them in quarters and parboiling them. They are left in the drainer in the sink. When she returns she adds the potatoes, salt, and pepper to the roast, and allows it to cook 30 minutes longer. The steaming hot roast is surrounded by the browned potatoes and served on a hot platter.

Me? Just now I have a chuck roast baking at 300° with a can of undiluted onion soup poured over it. The house smells like a well-seasoned feast is being prepared for the king's table. (Few things announce the preparation of a good meal like the aroma of cooking onions. Long ago someone told me that if the time for husband's return from work slips up on you and dinner isn't even started, just set a few plates and forks here and there and put a flower in the middle of the table and he will think you are well under way. I prefer to pop a pan on the stove and sauté an onion. He will come through the door saying, "Hmm-m, what's for dinner?" If you try this system, for gracious sake don't answer, "Who knows?" Just sniff the air and answer, "Hmm-m.")

In her book *Let's Cook It Right*, Adelle Davis speaks of the good, browned-meat flavor which is achieved by submitting meats to high temperatures. Contrary to the old belief that juices could be held in by searing, juices *do* spill, but they evaporate too quickly to be noticed. You should sear meats only with the aid of flour, crumbs, molasses, paprika, or sweetened fruit juices which brown easily.

Basting to keep meat moist is another bugaboo. Basting actually increases evaporation and dries the meat by washing off the fat. If you feel you must baste, baste with a pastry brush dipped in oil.

Another clue to flavorful cooking concerns salt. If you want the juices drawn out of the meat for tastier soup or gravy, salt the meat before cooking it. If you want the meat to be juicy, salt it just before eating it.[1]

---

[1] (New York: Harcourt, Brace & World, Inc., 1962), p. 20.

➤➤✷ MENU ✷◄◄

32

Beef Roast
  with Sweet and Sour Sauce
Rice
Molded Carrot Salad
Broiled Tomatoes
Hot Curried Fruit

Bread and Butter
Coffee, Tea, or Milk

Fix-Ahead Instructions

1. Cook roast and cut into 1½-inch cubes.
2. Prepare salad ingredients. Do not combine until just before serving.
3. Prepare fruit and have ready for oven.

Beef Roast with Sweet and Sour Sauce

Cut cooked roast into cubes. Before serving, pour 1 cup "Sweet and Sour Sauce" over cubes and bake at 350° for about 20 minutes. Serve on bed of instant rice, prepared according to directions on package.

Sweet and Sour Sauce

¼ cup tomato paste
1 cup water

3 T brown sugar
3 T vinegar

Combine all ingredients and cook over low fire 10 minutes.

("Sweet and Sour Sauce" can be bought at grocer's.)

Molded Carrot Salad

1 small pkg. apple gelatin
1 cup carrots, grated
¼ cup onion, minced
1 cup cabbage, shredded
¼ cup bell pepper, finely chopped

Prepare gelatin as directed on package. Add all other ingredients and pour into individual molds. Serve on lettuce leaf with mayonnaise.

Broiled Tomatoes

fresh tomatoes, ½ per person
1 cup sour cream
snipped parsley for garnish

Cut tomatoes in half through the equator, not through the north and south poles. Place 1 tablespoon sour cream on top of each half. Garnish with sprinkling of parsley. Put under broiler for just a minute.

Hot Curried Fruit

Make your own selection of fruit or use this list.

1 large can pears, drained
1 large can pineapple bits, drained
1 large can blue plums, seeded and drained
3 bananas, sliced

Sauce for fruit

1 stick margarine
¾ cup brown sugar
1½ tsp. curry powder

Make a sauce by combining ingredients and blending. Heat. Pour over fruit which has been drained and placed in a buttered casserole. Bake 30 to 45 minutes at 300°. Serve in your prettiest dessert bowls.

MENU

33

This is an easy-to-prepare cheese dinner.

Menu

Cheese-Rice Loaf	Bread and Butter
Applesauce Lemon Salad	Coffee, Tea, or Milk
Mint Carrots	
Angel Food Cake with Pat's Swirl Icing	

Fix-Ahead Instructions

1. Bake cheese-rice loaf ahead. Heat in oven in one pan placed in another pan of hot water. Or, place in oven with timer set for 1 hour at 325°.

Cheese-Rice Loaf

1 cup uncooked rice	½ cup parsley, chopped
¼ lb. American cheese, grated	2 eggs, slightly beaten
	1 cup milk
1 small onion, finely chopped	4 T margarine, melted

Mix all ingredients together and bake 1 hour at 325° in greased casserole set in pan of hot water. Any favorite sauce —mushroom, cheese, or spicy tomato—goes well with this, or it may be served alone.

Applesauce Lemon Salad

1 large pkg. lemon gelatin
1 cup water
1 small bottle 7-Up

1 can (2 cups) applesauce
pear halves, 1 per person

Prepare gelatin as directed but use only 1 cup hot water. Add 7-Up, applesauce, and mix. Pour over pear halves which have been placed in bottom of mold.

Mint Carrots

2 T margarine
1 tsp. cornstarch
1 T sugar
1 T mint leaves, shredded
  (dry or fresh)

⅓ cup water
1 T lemon juice
2 cups carrots, cooked
  (canned or frozen)

Melt margarine in pan. Add cornstarch and mix. Add sugar, shredded mint leaves, water, and lemon juice. Add the carrots to this mixture as it cooks. Remember this recipe as another mint dish to serve with lamb.

Angel Food Cake with Pat's Swirl Icing

1 angel food cake mix *or* ready-baked angel food cake

Icing

2 pkgs. pudding mix (any flavor), the no-cook variety
  (try lemon or chocolate)
2 cups milk
1 pint whipping cream

Prepare pudding mix according to directions on package, but use only ½ the amount of milk. This will be a total of 2 cups for the 2 packages of mix. In separate bowl whip the cream until stiff. Gently fold the whipped cream into the pudding. Cut cake into 3 layers and ice it. The frosting is of a soft consistency which lends itself to fancy swirling.

THANKSGIVING WEEK

"In every thing give thanks: for this is the will of God in Christ Jesus concerning you" (1 Thess. 5:18). Every day is a day of giving thanks, but during our historic week of Thanksgiving perhaps some of these suggestions may help you to be a little less hurried and a bit more thoughtful.

Cranberry Cocktail

1 bottle (16 oz.) cranberry juice cocktail
2 bottles (7 oz. each) ginger ale

Pour over finely crushed ice in a pitcher or punch bowl. Serve in juice glasses or punch cups. This makes about 8 juice-glass servings.

Tart Cranberry Salad

1 large pkg. raspberry gelatin
1 can cranberry sauce, with whole berries
½ medium orange with rind, run through food chopper
1 cup pecans

Prepare gelatin as directed. Add other ingredients. Mix and pour into mold.

Fresh and Canned Fruit with Catherine's Dressing

Try a big bowl of fresh and canned fruit, with "Catherine's

Dressing" placed in a pretty container nearby. This recipe makes one quart of dressing. You can keep it in the refrigerator for several weeks and serve with any canned or fresh fruit. You will be tempted to put it in a big cereal bowl and eat it with a spoon.

Catherine's Dressing

4 egg yolks	20 large marshmallows
4 T vinegar	½ pint whipping cream
4 T sugar	1 cup nuts, chopped
1 T prepared mustard	1 cup raisins

Combine egg yolks, vinegar, sugar, mustard, and marshmallows in double boiler or pan placed in another pan of hot water. Cook until melted and smooth. Add whipped cream, nuts, and raisins.

If you have misplaced your timetable for cooking turkey, perhaps this one will help. These times can be only approximate because of variation in types of roasters. Check toward the end of the prescribed cooking time to see how your turkey is progressing. If you like to tent-wrap your turkey with foil, the cooking time is reduced.

Weight of Turkey	Temperature	Approximate Time Required
6 to 9 lbs.	325°	2½ to 3 hours
10 to 13 lbs.	325°	3 to 4 hours
14 to 17 lbs.	300°	4½ to 5½ hours
18 to 25 lbs.	250° to 275°	6 to 8 hours

To test for doneness, take hold of turkey leg with paper towel. If the leg will move freely at the joint, the meat is cooked.

Nothing is so variable from family to family as stuffing recipes. This is where the cornbread girls and the non-cornbread girls, the egg girls and the non-egg girls, the prepared stuffing and the non-prepared stuffing girls draw the lines.

Let me just suggest a very basic recipe, and you can go on from there. Consider the addition of celery, apples, peanuts, almonds, mushrooms, oysters, raisins, and anything else that may occur to you. The base of most stuffings is formed of bread crumbs, cornbread, rice, crackers, or prepared stuffings. A combination of bases may be used.

Basic Stuffing Recipe

1 small onion, chopped
3 T margarine, melted
3 cups soft bread crumbs, or dry bread crumbs as preferred
1 tsp. salt
⅛ tsp. pepper
1 tsp. poultry seasoning
turkey broth to moisten to desired consistency

Chop onion and sauté in margarine until a delicate brown. Add bread crumbs and seasonings; mix. Add broth to make desired consistency. Bake in separate pan for 30 to 45 minutes. Stuff in turkey and bake, or place around turkey and bake. This is matter of personal preference. I am a separate-pan woman myself, and I like sage for seasoning.

Candied Sweet Potatoes

2 cans (1 lb. each) sweet potatoes, drained
marshmallows

Place sweet potatoes side by side in greased casserole. Pour syrup (see recipe below) over and bake 20 minutes at 400°, basting from time to time with syrup. Just before serving, place marshmallows on top and return to oven. Let brown lightly.

Syrup for Sweet Potatoes

⅔ cup brown sugar   1½ T margarine
¼ cup water   1 T light corn syrup

Combine ingredients. Boil 5 minutes. Pour hot over sweet potatoes. Return to oven.

For other garnishes try chopped nuts or white grapes sprinkled over in addition to marshmallows.

Potato Puffs

If your family would feel that you had been a traitor by deserting mashed potatoes and gravy with the turkey, by all means ignore this suggestion and go right on mashing. However, if they have no particular emotion on the subject, try potato puffs (p. 118) but omit the onion in the recipe. These can be placed around the edge of the turkey platter or served on a separate dish. They have the advantage of requiring no care at the last moment when a dozen things need to be done.

Standard Pumpkin Pie

1 unbaked pastry shell,
  9-inch

2 eggs, slightly beaten	½ tsp. ginger
1 can (#303) pumpkin	¼ tsp. cloves
¾ cup sugar	1⅔ cups evaporated milk, or
½ tsp. salt	light cream
1 tsp. cinnamon	

Mix ingredients in order given. Pour into pastry shell. Bake in hot oven (425°) for 15 minutes. Then reduce heat to 350° and continue baking 45 minutes. Test to see if the pie is done by inserting knife in center. If knife comes out clean the pie is done.

Garnishes for Pumpkin Pie

whipped cream
whipped cream with pecans or almonds sprinkled over
whipped cream with honey drizzled over
wedges of sharp cheddar cheese
toasted coconut

CHRISTMAS WEEK

"He came unto his own, and his own received him not. But as many as received him, to them gave he power to become the sons of God, even to them that believe on his name" (John 1: 11–12).

The happiness of the Christmas message expresses itself in many ways. For most families it is a season of being together. Perhaps some of the recipes given here will fit in with your traditional Christmas week as you prepare for your family and friends.

Favorite Cherry Coke Salad

1 large pkg. black cherry gelatin
1 large pkg. strawberry gelatin
2 cups boiling water
2 small bottled Cokes
2 pkgs. (3 oz. each) cream cheese
1 cup celery, finely diced
1 can (2 cups) crushed pineapple, drained
1 can (2 cups) Bing cherries, seeded and drained
1 cup nuts, coarsely chopped

Prepare gelatin by adding only 2 cups boiling water to the two packages. Add Cokes and chill until slightly thickened. Beat cream cheese until smooth and add fruits and nuts to it. Fold into gelatin. Chill until firm.

Walnut Lime Christmas Salad

1 large pkg. lime gelatin
½ pint whipping cream
1 can (2 cups) crushed pineapple, drained
¼ cup walnut pieces

Prepare gelatin with ⅓ less water for stiffer mold. When slightly thickened fold in whipped cream, pineapple, and walnuts. Refrigerate.

Anita's Frozen Fruit Salad

1 pkg. (8 oz.) cream cheese
¼ cup mayonnaise
1 can (2 cups) crushed pineapple, drained
1 bottle maraschino cherries, drained and cut up
½ pkg. miniature marshmallows
½ cup nuts
½ pint whipping cream

Beat cheese until smooth. Add mayonnaise, marshmallows, pineapple, cherries, and nuts. Fold in whipped cream last. Pour into ice tray and freeze. Allow to thaw slightly before serving.

Mrs. Lanier's Cranberry Jelly

4 cups cranberries
1½ cups water
2 cups sugar

Cook cranberries until they quit popping. Force them through a strainer. Add sugar. Bring to a full boil. Place in mold which has been rinsed in cold water. Refrigerate.

Carrington Broccoli Salad

2 pkgs. frozen broccoli,
  cooked but not well done
¼ cup mayonnaise

1 can consommé,
  undiluted
½ tsp. salt

½ cup sour cream
3 hard-boiled eggs, chopped
1 envelope unflavored
  gelatin

1 tsp. Worcestershire
  sauce
2 T lemon juice
few drops Tabasco

Cook broccoli. Mix mayonnaise and sour cream with chopped eggs. Dissolve gelatin in ¼ cup consommé and heat remainder of consommé to boiling. Add gelatin to this boiling liquid. Add all seasonings. Cool and add to mayonnaise and sour cream mixture. Lay cooked broccoli in bottom of mold or square pan and pour mixture over. Refrigerate overnight.

Mother-in-law's Chicken, Dressing, and Gravy Squares

This is an excellent dish to be carried across town to a pre-Christmas dinner at the church. (Be sure to bake this for your family ahead of time to try it out. There is nothing tricky about it, but it is a bit different from most recipes and if you have tried it and know just the right consistency for the gravy, you will be gay and confident on the day you pin on your Christmas corsage, take pan in hand, and leave the house.)

Gravy

4 T flour
1 cup chicken broth
4 eggs

1 quart milk
salt to taste

Beat eggs and stir into quart of milk. Make smooth paste of flour and 2 tablespoons of the broth. Add paste to remainder of broth and combine with egg and milk mixture. Add salt to taste. Cook 3 minutes over low flame.

Instructions for Combining

Line 9 by 13 by 2-inch pan or casserole with dressing about ½ inch thick to form a crust. Place cooked chicken cubes in this crust. Pour gravy over. Sprinkle top with layer of bread crumbs. Bake 30 minutes at 350°. Cut in squares to serve. This freezes well. One quart chicken serves about 12.

Mrs. Anderson's Crisp Date Cookies

1 stick margarine
1¾ cups sugar
1 lb. dates, cut in pieces

3 cups Rice Krispies
¾ cup nuts, broken

In large, heavy skillet melt margarine. Add sugar and dates and continue to heat, stirring constantly until dates dissolve and the mixture becomes smooth. Add Rice Krispies and nuts. Allow to cool slightly. Shape into long rolls and wrap in waxed paper. Refrigerate and slice as needed. These do not require baking. They will stay fresh for several weeks.

Suzanne's Sugar Cookies

½ stick margarine
¼ cup butter
1 cup sugar
1 tsp. vanilla

2 eggs
2½ cups sifted flour
½ tsp. baking powder
1 tsp. cinnamon

Cream sugar and shortening. Add vanilla and eggs and beat until light. Measure flour after sifting. Sift dry ingredients 3 times. Add to creamed mixture and mix. Wrap in wax paper and chill for 2 hours or place in freezer 20 minutes. Roll thin and cut with floured cutter. Bake on greased cookie sheet 8 to 10 minutes at 400°. Cool and sprinkle with sugar.

Rocky Road Chips

1 cup semisweet chocolate bits
¾ cup miniature marshmallows
1½ cup coarsely crushed corn chips

Melt chocolate chips in double boiler. Remove from heat. Stir in marshmallows and corn chips. Stir lightly with fork until all is coated with chocolate. Use 2 forks to pick up small mounds and place on buttered surface. Refrigerate.

Can't Fail Fudge

2¼ cups sugar
¾ cup evaporated milk

⅛ cup light corn syrup
2 T margarine
2 cups semisweet chocolate bits
2 tsp. vanilla
1 cup raisins, chopped nuts, or coconut (optional)

Combine sugar, evaporated milk, corn syrup, and butter in saucepan. Bring to a boil, stirring constantly. Cook over moderate heat for 5 minutes continuing to stir. Add chocolate bits and vanilla and stir until smooth. Add raisins, nuts, or coconut if you like. Cool on buttered plate.

Fudge Squares

This is a recipe for people who just cannot make fudge, not even "Can't Fail Fudge." It won't fail to get hard for the simple reason that it is hard at the beginning. It will be very thick as you work with it. Taste after you mix it and add more vanilla if you like. If it is too thick to work with, add milk very, very sparingly.

4 squares (4 ozs.) baking chocolate, melted	1 lb. powdered sugar, sifted
1 egg	5 T milk
1 tsp. margarine, melted	1 T vanilla
¼ cup nuts	

Melt chocolate over hot water and remove from fire. Add unbeaten egg. Stir for 1 minute. Add melted margarine and sugar alternately with milk. This will be very thick. Add vanilla. Press into refrigerator tray or other pan of similar size. Sprinkle nuts over top. Makes 1 ice tray of very thick fudge or 1½ trays of medium thickness. Chill for several hours.

"Christmas itself may be called into question/If carried so far it creates indigestion," rhymed Ralph Bergengren. Just a cheerful thought before giving you this recipe.

Eyre Heavenly Hash

7 5-cent chocolate Hershey bars	*Yes, dear!*
4 oz. pkg. semisweet chocolate bits	*Dare you go on?*
¼ cup water	*There, that's sensible.*
5 eggs, separated	*Just as nourishing as breakfast—*
⅓ cup sugar	*A reasonable amount . . .*
1 tsp. vanilla	*Everything requires vanilla.*
2 cups chopped nuts	*There's a many caloried thing.*
1 large angel food cake	*Sounds innocuous.*

Melt candy bars and chocolate bits in water over low heat.
Add five beaten egg yolks and cool.

Beat 5 egg whites stiff and add sugar slowly.

Add vanilla and nuts to chocolate mixture.

Fold in egg whites.

Break cake into bite-sized pieces. In tube pan place layer of cake pieces and layer of chocolate mixture. Repeat.

Refrigerate overnight. Remove from pan. Slice and add whipped cream if you like.

Then, put on dish and go up and down block serving to everyone who weighs less than 100 pounds with shoes on.

Sister's Can't Fail Applesauce Cake

I wanted to put this recipe in just as I received it from my sister back in the days when all the children were babies, and we were looking for recipes that called for exactly what was in the pantry so no unscheduled trips to the grocery store would need to be made. Wrapped well, this cake can be kept several weeks and will still be moist. Or, it can be frozen. It can become one of the sections of the backbone of your Christmas baking—the kind to have already tucked away before you begin your fancy baking.

½ cup shortening	Cream well.
2 cups sugar	

1 egg	Add and beat. (If you don't have
2 cups applesauce	applesauce on hand, just cut up 3
2½ cups sifted flour	apples and cook in ½ cup water
2 tsp. soda	while you cream the other ingredi-
1 tsp. cinnamon	ents.)
1 tsp. allspice	
1 tsp. cloves	Add. (You may use any spices you
1 tsp. salt	have if you don't have these.)
juice from ½ lemon	(If you don't have one or the other
juice from ½ orange	of these, use the whole of either or
	an extract.)

¼ cup flour	Add last. (Substitute candied fruit
2 cups raisins	for part of raisins. Mix these into
1 cup nuts	flour before adding so they won't
1 tsp. vanilla	settle to the bottom.)

Wilba's Chocolate Pound Cake

Even if you are not a cake-maker, try this recipe. It makes a big, beautiful cake—all your tube pan will hold—and it has a texture which is truly like velvet.

2 sticks margarine	2 tsp. baking powder
½ cup vegetable shortening	½ cup cocoa
3 cups sugar	½ tsp. salt
5 eggs	1¼ cups milk
3 cups flour	1 T vanilla

Cream margarine and shortening, adding sugar gradually. Add eggs one at a time, beating well after each addition. Sift together the flour, baking powder, cocoa, and salt *three times*. (You will be tempted not to do this, but do. It is one of the reasons for the delightful texture of this cake.) Add to mixture alternately with the milk. Add vanilla. Pour batter into tube pan that has been greased and dusted with flour. Bake at

300° for about 2 hours with a pan of water in the bottom of the oven.

Anita's Rice Casserole

This casserole is very useful in those days after Christmas when there is lots of drop-in company for meals and the turkey is already past history.

1 cup uncooked rice
2 cups water
1 can consommé
⅔ cup margarine

1 can water chestnuts *or*
1 cup pecans
½ tsp. salt

Put raw rice in casserole. In separate pot combine water, consommé, and margarine. Bring to a boil. Add salt and nuts and pour over rice. Cover and bake at 350° for 1 hour.

Punch for a family occasion often adds a special note. I think few children ever forget that the punch bowl was gotten out for their birthday. Here are some simple recipes.

Ginger Ale with Sherbet

1 large bottle ginger ale
1 quart sherbet

Pour bottle of ginger ale into punch bowl and add sherbet which you have separated into several pieces. (The sherbet will slowly melt and separate into smaller pieces.) Serve in punch cups, being sure there is a bit of sherbet in each cup. Use any flavor of sherbet your family likes best or match the color scheme of your table. (If you are using a glass punch bowl, avoid placing the frozen sherbet in the bowl before you have poured in the ginger ale, or you risk cracking your bowl.) You may substitute one of the bottled punches for ginger ale if you like.

Spiced Pineapple Punch (Hot or Iced)

2 cups water
¼ cups sugar
3 cinnamon sticks, broken
1 tsp. whole cloves
1 large can pineapple juice

Boil water, sugar, cinnamon sticks, and cloves together for 10 minutes. Strain and mix with pineapple juice. Serve hot on a cold Christmas Eve or pour over crushed ice any time and serve as a cold punch.

Fruit Punch

pear nectar
apricot nectar
orange juice
ginger ale

Combine equal parts of each. Mix and serve over crushed ice.

Frosty Cider

1 bottle apple cider or juice
1 quart orange sherbet

Add scoops of orange sherbet to apple cider.

Tart Punch

orange juice or lemonade, canned
grape juice

Combine equal parts of juices and serve over crushed ice.

✠✠ MENU ✠✠

34

Don't hesitate to cook Swiss steak ahead and heat before serving if this fits best with your schedule.

Menu

Swiss Steak   Bread and Butter
Easy Potato Puffs   Coffee, Tea, or Milk
  with Onion Seasoning
Celery with Shrimp Stuffing
Chocolate Pie in Coconut
  Crust

Fix-Ahead Instructions

1. Cook steak a day ahead, or, on Sunday morning brown steak and add seasonings. Place in oven with timer set for 1½ hours.
2. Prepare potato puffs, but do not bake until just before serving.
3. Prepare celery with shrimp stuffing. Refrigerate.
4. Prepare pie. Refrigerate.

Swiss Steak

2 lbs. round steak,   1 tsp. salt
  1 inch thick   ¼ tsp. pepper
¼ cup flour   1 can (6 oz.) tomato paste
2 T margarine   1 cup water
2 cups onions, sliced

Pound flour into meat with edge of heavy saucer. Brown steak on both sides. Brown onions in separate pan. Cover meat with onions. Add salt, pepper, tomato paste, and water. Cook covered over low heat or bake at 350° about 1 hour.

Easy Potato Puffs with Onion Seasoning

instant potatoes (servings for 4 to 6)
1 medium onion, chopped fine

Do try these. This is my favorite way to serve potatoes to guests when I don't want to have any last-minute chores. Prepare instant potatoes as directed on package. Add the minced onion. With a serving spoon lift potato portions the size of an egg and place them on a cookie sheet. Shape and smooth portions with the spoon and make peaks on top. Brush lightly with margarine and dash with paprika. Place under broiler until lightly browned, or bake 10 to 20 minutes at 350°.

Celery with Shrimp Stuffing

1 can (4½ oz.) shrimp, chopped fine
1 pkg. (3 oz.) cream cheese
2 T mayonnaise
1 tsp. onion, minced
1 tsp. parsley, chopped
dash of Worcestershire sauce

Prepare celery and cut diagonally in 3-inch sections. Combine above ingredients and stuff celery sections.

Chocolate Pie in Coconut Crust

Coconut Crust

½ stick margarine
¼ cup sugar
1½ cups shredded coconut

Combine ingredients in heavy pan and cook over low heat, stirring constantly until golden brown. Turn quickly into pie pan and press into crust shape.

Pie Filling

1 box chocolate pudding-and-pie filling
½ pint whipping cream

Prepare chocolate mix as directed on box. Fold in cream which
has been whipped until it stands in peaks. Refrigerate.

➤❈ MENU ❈⬅

35

With thought and a bit of experimenting to discover the exact taste of your individual family, meat loaf can become a specialty of the house. Hot meat loaf just from the oven is a pleasant, cold winter's day dish. Leftover meat loaf, sliced and broiled with a dot of butter on each piece, is a delight when served at breakfast with eggs and chilled fruit. Below is a meal built around meat loaf with hot onion sauce.

White sauce is the basis of this onion sauce. If you are not a white-sauce expert, do master the very uncomplicated art because this sauce is the base for many cream soups, creamed vegetables, creamed diced meats, creamed hard-boiled eggs, and so on. It is also the base for many of the French sauces, some of which require no more than the addition of whipped egg yolks and the substitution of cream for milk in your white sauce recipe.

White Sauce (thin)

1 T margarine	1 cup milk
1 T flour	salt to taste

Melt margarine. Add flour and blend. Add milk and cook slowly, stirring until thickened. Salt to taste.

Broiled Meat Loaf Slices
 with Onion Sauce
Tomatoes Stuffed with
 Macaroni Salad
Carrots
Praline Apple Pie

Brown Bread and Butter
Coffee, Tea, or Milk

Fix-Ahead Instructions

1. Prepare and bake meat loaf a day ahead. Prepare onion sauce also a day ahead. Refrigerate.

2. Prepare tomatoes and stuff a day ahead. Cover and refrigerate.

3. Prepare apple pie. Serve pie cold with heated topping, or spoon topping over pie and heat about 15 minutes in warm oven while family is eating main course.

Broiled Meat Loaf Slices with Onion Sauce

Prepare and bake meat loaf, using your own recipe (or see page 70). When cool, slice meat loaf and arrange on serving dish which can be placed under broiler. Refrigerate. Before serving allow to come to room temperature. Then run meat loaf slices under broiler to heat through.

Onion Sauce

2 cups white sauce (thin)
1 medium onion, minced
1 tsp. monosodium glutamate
2 tsp. parsley flakes
2 hard-boiled eggs, diced

1 small can pimiento, cut up
1 small can mushroom pieces, drained

Combine all ingredients and heat. Pour over hot meat loaf slices as they come from broiler.

Tomatoes Stuffed with Macaroni Salad

Select medium-sized tomatoes and cut in half, cutting as you would a grapefruit, not through the stem end. Remove centers (reserve to add to salad at another meal) to form tomato cups. Fill with macaroni salad.

Macaroni Salad

2 cups shell macaroni, cooked	2 T onion, minced
½ cup mayonnaise	1 cup celery, diced
2 tsp. prepared mustard	¼ cup sweet pickle relish
	½ cup stuffed olives

Cook macaroni as directed on package. Cool. Blend seasonings with mayonnaise until smooth. Add to macaroni and mix. Place in tomato cups.

Carrots

To a can or package of frozen carrots add 2 tablespoons margarine, 1 tablespoon sugar and ½ teaspoon cinnamon. Cook.

Apple Pie with Praline Topping

Buy a prepared apple pie or make your own. Add "Praline Topping."

Praline Topping

2 T honey	1 egg, beaten
½ cup brown sugar	½ tsp. vanilla
2 T margarine	½ cup pecans

Combine honey, brown sugar, and margarine, and bring to a boil. Add about 2 tablespoons of the boiling liquid to beaten egg and blend until smooth. (This is to prevent the egg from cooking too quickly.) Return egg mixture to honey and brown sugar mixture. Continue to boil for 1 minute. Add nuts. Serve hot over cool pie or spoon over warm pie.

➤❄ MENU ❄◄

36

No dish is better designed to keep a busy mother out of a stew than a hearty stew.

Menu

Beef Stew
  with Collar of Mashed
  Potatoes
Green Salad
Broiled Tomatoes with
  Cheese
Ice Cream Pie

Brown Bread and Butter
Coffee, Tea, or Milk

Fix-Ahead Instructions

1. Cook stew ahead. Heat and add mashed potato collar just before serving.
2. Prepare greens for salad ahead and refrigerate.
3. Arrange tomato halves in broiler-proof dish. Do not broil until just before serving.
4. Prepare ice cream pie ahead and freeze.

Beef Stew with Collar of Mashed Potatoes

2 lbs. stew meat or chunks
  of inexpensive cut of beef
2 T margarine

3 T flour
1 tsp. monosodium glutamate
4 large onions

1 tsp. salt   6 carrots
¼ tsp. pepper   1 cup celery, chopped

Instant potatoes to be used for collar

In large kettle brown stew meat or roast which has been cut into 1-inch squares and sprinkled with salt, pepper, and flour. Add water to cover, and simmer about 45 minutes. Add prepared vegetables. Add more water, salt, and pepper as needed. Simmer until meat is tender and vegetables are done.

For potato collar prepare instant potatoes for 5 to 6 servings as directed on package. Place these on top of stew around edge of pan to form ornamental collar. With spoon shape into peaks. Brush with margarine and dot with paprika. Run under broiler or in oven until peaks of potatoes are lightly browned.

Green Salad

½ head lettuce
2 ribs celery, sliced
4 slices bacon, cooked and crumbled
1 carrot, cut in small pieces

Combine ingredients and add your favorite dressing.

Broiled Tomatoes with Cheese

Cut tomatoes in half, allowing ½ tomato per person. Lay over each half a slice of cheese just large enough to cover and barely drape over. Run under broiler until cheese just bubbles.

Ice Cream Pie

baked pie shell or graham cracker shell
1 pint ice cream
¼ pint whipping cream
¼ cup frozen strawberries (or other fruit)
3 drops red food coloring

This pie is very showy and easy to fix.
Slightly soften ice cream until you can work with it. Place it

inside the prepared crust, pressing it against crust to form filling for pie. Leave hole in center about the size of a tea cup. Return to freezer. Whip ½ pint whipping cream and add to it bits of frozen or fresh fruit. Color cream mixture slightly with red food coloring. (If you don't color the whipped cream mixture, there is not enough contrast between the ice cream and whipped cream.) Place colored fruit-cream mixture in center opening of pie. Garnish with bits of fruit. Return to freezer. Allow to thaw about 10 minutes before serving.

⇥➤❊ MENU ❊⇤

37

This is a colorful all vegetable dinner with a rich dessert.

Menu

Green Rice
Tomato Sandwich Salad
Corn Broccoli Bake
Rich Chocolate Cake

Bread
Coffee, Tea, or Milk

Fix-Ahead Instructions

1. Combine all "Green Rice" ingredients except the rice itself. Do not add rice until ready to bake.
2. Cook eggs for "Tomato Sandwich Salad."
The assembling of the "Tomato Sandwich Salad" is a job which needs to be done just before serving. Since it requires no high level of skill, instruct one of the children and let them do this job. Leave your hands free for the "Green Rice" preparation.
3. Assemble "Corn Broccoli Bake" and have it ready for the oven.
4. Bake chocolate cake ahead.

Green Rice

2 cups uncooked instant rice
2 cups sharp cheese, grated
1 large onion, chopped

1 pkg. frozen chopped spinach, cooked
½ tsp. salt

126

1 cup milk   ½ cup margarine,
2 eggs, beaten   melted

Cook instant rice as directed on package. Add all other ingredients, which have already been combined. Mix lightly. Bake at 350° for 30 to 45 minutes in a greased casserole.

Tomato Sandwich Salad

Make a sandwich for each person, using slices of tomato, lettuce, and hard-boiled egg placed between as filling. Dot top with mayonnaise. Add a sprig of parsley.

Corn Broccoli Bake

1 can whole kernel corn,   1 cup milk
   drained   1 egg, well beaten
1 pkg. frozen broccoli,   1 can water chestnuts
   cooked   (optional)
2 T flour
2 T margarine

In greased casserole alternate layers of corn and cooked broccoli. In separate pan make sauce by melting margarine, adding flour, and blending. Add milk and cook over low heat until slightly thickened. Add water chestnuts to sauce. Pour over corn and broccoli in casserole. Bake for 15 minutes.

Rich Chocolate Cake

2 cups flour   1 cup water
2 cups sugar   ½ cup buttermilk
1 stick margarine   1 tsp. soda
½ cup vegetable shortening   2 eggs, slightly beaten
4 T cocoa   1 tsp. vanilla

Sift flour and sugar together in mixing bowl. In separate pan combine margarine, vegetable shortening, cocoa, and water and bring to hard boil. Pour boiling mixture over flour and sugar. Combine buttermilk and soda and stir into chocolate

mixture. Beat in eggs and vanilla. When well mixed, pour into greased rectangular pan. Bake 20 minutes at 400°.
Start frosting 5 minutes before cake is done.

Frosting

1 stick margarine
4 T cocoa
6 T milk

1 box powdered sugar, sifted
1 cup pecans
¼ tsp. vanilla

Combine margarine, cocoa, and milk, and bring to a boil. Add powdered sugar, pecans, and vanilla. Beat until proper consistency to spread on cake. Spread while still warm.